🖤🖤🖤

LEARNING TO KNOW GOD

🖤🖤🖤

...and to Love His Friends

🖤🖤🖤

Devotional Daybooks
By Neva Coyle

Learning to Know God
Making Sense of Pain and Struggle
Meeting the Challenges of Change
A New Heart . . . A New Start

A Devotional Daybook

by Neva Coyle

❦❦❦

LEARNING TO KNOW GOD

❦❦❦

...and to Love His Friends

❦❦❦

BETHANY HOUSE PUBLISHERS
MINNEAPOLIS, MINNESOTA 55438

Published by Bethany House Publishers
A Ministry of Bethany Fellowship, Inc.
11300 Hampshire Avenue South
Minneapolis, Minnesota 55438

Printed in the United States of America

Library of Congress Cataloging-in-Publication Data

Coyle, Neva, 1943–
    Learning to know God / Neva Coyle.
        p. cm. — (A Devotional daybook)
    1. Meditations. I. Title. II. Series: Coyle, Neva, 1943–   Devotional
daybook.
BV4832.2.C678   1993
242—dc20   93–23320
ISBN 1–55661–339–3   CIP

To Sandy

♡

NEVA COYLE is Founder of Overeaters Victorious and President of Neva Coyle Ministries. Presently she is the Coordinator of Departmental Ministries in her church. Her ministry is enhanced by her bestselling books and tapes, as well as by her being a gifted motivational speaker/teacher. Neva and her husband make their home in California.

She may be contacted at:

P.O. Box 2330
Orange, CA 92669

Preface

HOW MANY CHRISTIANS really know the full potential of the richness of their relationship with Christ? How many experience full and satisfying relationships with others? How many feel strong enough to reach out to a stranger sitting next to them on the bus or in front of them at church? How many of us know the pains carried by the person working at the next desk? Some who have experienced salvation feel second-class because of early childhood conditioning; some consider their lives a waste and themselves a failure. Many barely hang on from week to week because of emotional injury, having no understanding of their individual worth.

John 15—an inviting passage—speaks of being fully united in Christ to the point that there is no life apart from Him and no accomplishment without Him. It tells us that in Him— abiding in Him—life is marked by fullness, affirmation, and purpose; in Christ we can feel as if we belong and feel comfortable among His friends. His promise is one of assurance, love, and victory.

Years ago I wrote a short Bible study based on this theme. I now expand the concept of "abiding," further exploring our relationship with the Father, through His Son, Jesus.

It is my prayer that as you work through this study in your

quiet time, you will take its principles into your everyday life—into your human relationships. You see, a life united with Christ, a life reconciled with God the Father, is also a life of ever-maturing human relationships.

This could very well be a turning point in your life as you learn more about abiding—building relationship with God and also with His friends.

Contents

How to Use This Book

THIS DEVOTIONAL STUDY is designed to fit easily into a busy schedule. It is divided into six sections, with five entries in each section. By reading an entry each day, you can complete the study in just thirty days. Take a few minutes each day to read the suggested Scripture and accompanying thought. Apply the Scripture selection to your life by answering the questions at the end of each entry. Writing your own response in the space after questions will help you better establish the scriptural truths in your life.

If the book is used in a group study, members can study the five entries of a section during the week and then meet as a group to discuss the material. In this way the book will take six weeks to complete or longer, depending on the needs of the group. The study is easily adaptable to an established women's ministry group or a Sunday school class.

For groups using the study, I've included suggested leader's guidelines and discussion questions at the end of the book.

Section I

The Challenge of Change

If you remain in me and my words remain in you, ask whatever you wish, and it will be given you. This is to my Father's glory, that you bear much fruit, showing yourselves to be my disciples. As the Father has loved me, so have I loved you. Now remain in my love.

JOHN 15:7–9

COME LIVE IN relationship with me. Stay right here, near me; experience my love. Sit right here beside me. Settle yourself in my promises. Put down stakes in my presence. Plant yourself in my Word.

All these phrases are so inviting, yes?

Well, maybe not.

Such words of invitation can be threatening. When we hide in personal fortresses, behind self-built walls, barricades, and barriers, it can be difficult if not impossible to accept Jesus' invitation to experience a full relationship with Him.

We wish we felt we could trust Him, but we've been hurt before, so it feels safe to hide behind the emotional blockades.

We erect barriers to intimacy and then grieve over our loneliness. Dug in behind our barricades, we cry, "Where is God?"

Is there any way out of our formidable fortresses into warm relationship with God?

Yes. He has invited us into relationship with Him, and in a curious way that relationship starts as we give Him an invitation to come into our lives. Fellowship with God can happen only when we have the courage to tear down the walls from the inside and let Him in. Let Him love you. Tear down the walls.

Chapter
· 1 ·

Breaking Down the Barriers

By faith the walls of Jericho fell, after the people had marched around them for seven days.

Hebrews 11:30

HUDDLED SAFELY in a dark corner underneath stacks of boxes, the scared kitten refused to be coaxed out.

"Here, kitty, kitty," we called. We tried to entice her with warm milk. We wiggled a piece of string thinking she might pounce, so we could grab hold of her. But no. She wouldn't accept our overtures. She drank the milk we put out only after we'd left the premises. Otherwise she stayed huddled safely behind her barricades, waiting for us to leave so she would feel secure enough to accept our provision.

We were confident that she *would* respond once she learned we were her friends, her loving providers. And, yes, in time, when she could trust us, we were able to persuade her to let us touch her and finally hold her.

This little patchwork kitten, her gray eyes staring at me from her safe enclave—out of my reach—reminded me of how I have been suspicious of God, afraid to get too close.

It seems safer and far more comfortable to look at Him from my "fortress" even as I depend on His provision. Born again? Sure. Member of a good church? Of course. Personal relationship with Jesus Christ? Well, sort of.

You can pray, read the Bible, and even go to a women's group or men's prayer breakfast and settle for activity that *looks* as if you are living in relationship with God, all the while keeping the barricades up. You can be around Christians, mouth worship songs, and still avoid closeness with Him.

We can get so used to being a distant relative of the Lord that we become satisfied with much less than what He offers. "Here I am!" Jesus says. "I stand at the door and knock. If anyone hears my voice and opens the door, I will come in and eat with him, and he with me" (Revelation 3:20).

Thinking of this verse, I once said to a friend, "You know, I have no doubt that I will go to heaven. I can imagine myself at the Marriage Supper of the Lamb, yet I have trouble believing that I would ever be invited to have lunch with Jesus."

In the forty years I have known and served the Lord, I have never sensed His challenging me to come as close to Him as in recent months. In my prayer times I hear Him whisper to my lonely heart, "Unlock the door. I am waiting for your invitation to come in."

Are you hearing the same invitation? Are you safely entrenched in your doctrines, your Christian lifestyle, yet all the while keep your safe distance from your Abba Father, your Papa God?

He isn't going to crash through the barriers, smash the barricades, or scale the walls you've erected. He is a gentleman. He calls at the door and waits to be invited in. Can you risk it? Can I? Do you have the courage? Do I? Will we step out in faith and, like Joshua, let the walls fall and let Him in? Do we dare?

Name the biggest barrier that you've erected between you and the Lord.

If you were in a small room with Jesus, would you feel threatened? By what?

If you were to answer the door and find Jesus standing there,
what words would you say to invite Him in? Write them:

What would you say if He brought along a friend of His whom
you didn't quite approve of?

Chapter
· 2 ·

Getting
Acquainted

*For God so loved the world that he gave his one and only
Son, that whoever believes in him shall not perish but
have eternal life. For God did not send his Son into the
world to condemn the world, but to save the world
through him.*

John 3:16–17

IF YOU'RE LIKE most people, you probably have asked questions along these lines when you've met someone new:

"Who is she?"

"What does he do?"

"What's she like?"

"What does he want?"

Conditioned by sour experiences, we approach each new person we meet with a certain amount of reserve and "guardedness."

We're suspicious of clinging or controlling types—men and women who offer friendship with ulterior motives. We've had enough of miserly, self-serving friendships. We've let one too many opportunistic people into our lives. We're smarter now. We ask the important questions *first* and love later—maybe.

But when all the care and concern we take in forming new

relationships does not protect us from men on the make or women who look only to their own interests and questionable needs, we withdraw further. Fearful, we pull away and become more alone than ever.

And we are so bound by our human experiences that we compare the relationship God offers to us with the human relationships we have been offered in the past: relationships marred by polluted motives and scarred by wounds that don't heal.

It's no wonder that when God approaches us open-handed and open-hearted, we tend to doubt and wonder about His motives. After all, what's in this relationship for Him? What does He want of me?

No wonder we think God's love is strange and His offered opportunity for relationship peculiar. We measure it by former offers of human love. When we equate "love" with the pain of rejection, criticism, and manipulation, we decide we'll not be duped again. But when we compare the relationship God offers to us with controlling human relationships, we are doomed to be the losers.

You see, God's love is not a variation, not a different version of the love you have experienced in the past. His love is true. It is real, good, and uncorrupted. His love is the pure love you have been longing for. It is unmixed with self-serving human agendas. God's love is unmingled with egotistical self-interest. God's love is flawless, faultless, and holy. Not like anything you've ever experienced before. Sound incredible?

But there's more. Remember when you spent long hours of empty effort trying to earn the little love you got in human relationships? God's love is given—freely. You can't earn it. You can't ever hope to be good enough to deserve it. You can't make yourself holy enough to merit His love. You can't give enough of yourself or your money to buy it. It's given.

Think about it: For God so loved that he gave. . . . Wow. Awesome. Shattering.

All my "buts" are silenced. All my defenses fall. All my doubts are overwhelmed. All my longings lie open. This love leaves me totally vulnerable in the safest sense, before the living God who loves me more than I could ever love Him.

And in that holy place of total peace and openness He

teaches me four important things:
1. He loves me—*no ifs, no buts, no conditions.*
2. He gave His Son, Jesus, to die *for me.*
3. All He asks in return is that I believe in the atoning work of His Son.
4. He offers me a relationship with Him in which His life flows through my life, and my life finds its meaning in Him.

The Ruler of the universe is a lover of people—you and me. He offers us His life, and we—well, it's up to us now, isn't it? We either take it or . . . Well, I've chosen to take it; how about you?

———

Write out John 3:16, inserting your own name at every appropriate point:

How is the relationship God offers different than relationships you've had in the past?

What is it about having a personal relationship with God that gives you hope?

How is that hope different from hope you've felt before?

Chapter
· 3 ·

No Strings
Attached

The LORD appeared to us in the past, saying:
"I have loved you with an everlasting love;
I have drawn you with loving-kindness."

Jeremiah 31:3

YOU'VE MET HER. She's the woman across the street who arrived with her basket of cookies before the movers could even put the furniture in your new house.

"Hi, I'm your new neighbor from down the way. I thought you might like a little refreshment—and a friendly face." Smiling ear to ear, she holds out a basket.

That first day she doesn't knock—a pattern that doesn't change.

"Good morning," she calls the next day as you take the moving cartons out to the curb. She heads your way with her coffee carafe in hand. "I made some gourmet coffee. Thought you probably hadn't made it to the store yet." She whisks into the kitchen without invitation and heads for the cupboards. "Where are the mugs?"

The shimmering gossamer threads of the day-old relationship threaten to become a net. The taste of yesterday's cookies is suddenly in your mouth.

You were planning to go back to bed once the empty boxes were at the curb. You've had it, traveling in the station wagon three days with two kids, a dog, and a chattering parakeet. You arrived barely an hour before the movers. You're not coping well with the furniture placement and the hundreds of boxes.

"I bet you're tired," she sympathizes.

"Well, I am pretty tired. I was planning—"

"You don't have to tell me. I've moved across country myself." She stands.

She's leaving! you think.

"Say, nice furniture you've got here. I didn't fare so well when I moved."

Oh, no, she's not leaving!

After twenty minutes of uninvited horror stories of her moving experiences, she looks at her watch. "I can stay only a little longer. I can't be late for the bridge club in my old neighborhood. We still get together once a week, you know, just for old times' sake."

An hour later you have reluctantly accepted a second cup of coffee, even though you knew the caffeine from the first would ruin any chance you had of a midmorning nap.

This budding friendship needs to be nipped, right there before it takes over your whole life like crabgrass in the backyard. You already feel smothered. Hiding behind pulled shades and not answering the phone before 10:30 only brings her to the back door "concerned" that you might not be well—"or something."

When this scenario happens to us again and again, we become shy of anyone who courts our attention and proposes a relationship. Sadly, burned by driven people who would coerce us into relationship with gifts and kindnesses all the while drawing us deeper into their nets of guilt and obligation, we suspect God of similar motives when He speaks to us of living in relationship with Him. Even when we read words like those above from Jeremiah 31:3, we hold ourselves erect, raise our eyebrows, and in so many ways and words say, *What do You mean by that?*

God says He loves me.

But I've heard that before from others who wanted only to own me.

26

God says He wants me close to Him.

I've heard that before, too, and it meant stifling possessiveness.

What's the difference between what God offers and what others have offered in the past?

What God offers is an invitation to relationship. Then He stands at a distance to let us see and be attracted to Him—rather than forcing a relationship based on His attraction to us. His offer is not a demand but an opportunity. He reaches out to us with cords of love, acts of kindness—not spiderwebs of duty, cables of obligation, and nets of guilt.

The lovely things God offers are closeness without confinement, relationship full of release and freedom. He offers us love—but with liberty.

In relationship with Him you can live uninhibited in worship; your prayer life can take on a dimension of openness and safe vulnerability. God never entraps; He emancipates.

Let Him woo you. God wants to have an intimate relationship with you; He loves you. But unless you are ready and accept His invitation, you don't have to worry—because He won't force you.

———

Recall an experience when someone "invaded" your life. Why was it difficult to get free from that relationship?

What are some of your reservations about becoming closer to God?

How are those reservations based on your experience with past human relationships rather than on your experience with or knowledge of God?

What does Jeremiah 31:3 say to you about the relationship God desires to have with you?

Chapter · 4 ·

Taking Root

*I pray that out of his glorious riches he may
strengthen you with power through his Spirit in your
inner being, so that Christ may dwell in your hearts
through faith. And I pray that you, being rooted and
established in love, may have power, together with all the
saints, to grasp how wide and long and high and deep is
the love of Christ, and to know this love that surpasses
knowledge—that you may be filled to the measure of all
the fullness of God.*

Ephesians 3:16–19

IMAGINE A LOVELY bouquet of fresh spring flowers deliv-
ered to your door and placed on your dining room table.

See how they brighten the entire room. Notice the pleas-
ant smiles when others pass by and look at the lovely arrange-
ment.

Such enjoyment, such color, so alive—so sadly temporary.

One day you see the green iris leaves turn a sickly shade
of brown, and soon the vibrant purple blossoms are a dull gray.
Something so alive, now dead. Once so pretty, now so tragic.
Only a nostalgic reminder of a special occasion or thoughtful
friend.

But it's no wonder the flowers—even leaves—died. They have been separated from their roots. Confined in a glass container and fed only water, the cuttings starved to death.

Not like my mom's garden iris. Cultivated, watered, and root-fed, the green, budded spires shoot some five feet into the fresh spring air, eventually exploding into huge blossoms. And then an unseen miracle occurs deep within the earth: The bulbs replenish and multiply, reproducing deliciously rich-colored flowers year after year.

How about you? Would you compare yourself to a cut flower or a planted one? A blossom placed on a table or one planted in the earth? Someone who temporarily splashes enjoyment and pleasure for those passing by or someone who flourishes, survives the seasonal changes, and produces faithfully year after year—a great satisfaction to the gardener?

As Christians we were designed to be planted—to live *in* relationship with God not merely to sit *on* a pew. We are meant to grow, to thrust our roots deep into the rich soil of God's love, nourished from underneath by His mercy and grace. We are intended to flourish and blossom again and again. We have been created to thrive and reproduce.

But we can live this rich, reproductive life only as we are established in, rooted in, Him. Settled in Him, we can live lodged in His presence, entrenched in His love, grounded in His Word with our identities based in His purpose for our lives.

Only *in* Him will we ever find the security, protection, and shelter we long for. Our lives will be stably anchored when we are securely fixed *in* Him.

In Him—and He *in* us. Surrounded by Him. In a relationship with Him, our position in Him secure. Not "on His arm" but *in* His heart. Not hanging on Him but abiding *in* Him.

Only then can we experience His peace and realize the satisfaction that comes from being "rooted and established in love." Only then can we begin to "have power, together with all the saints, to grasp how wide and long and high and deep is the love of Christ."

Then, through the seasons of life, through stages when we may not be in full bloom, our roots can always be reaching deeper, even reproducing, always with the assurance that we will blossom again—in the right season.

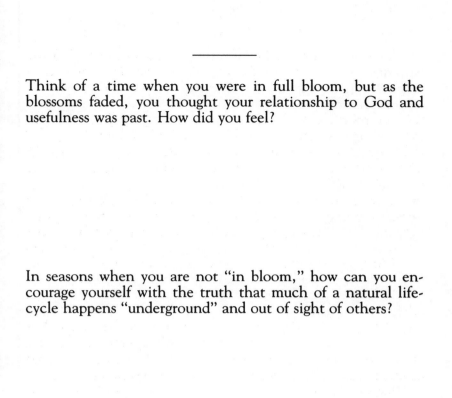

Think of a time when you were in full bloom, but as the blossoms faded, you thought your relationship to God and usefulness was past. How did you feel?

In seasons when you are not "in bloom," how can you encourage yourself with the truth that much of a natural life-cycle happens "underground" and out of sight of others?

What are some of the ways you can "cultivate" your own roots for deepening and reproducing?

What "season" in your relationship with the Lord are you currently in?
- planting
- germinating
- deep-root feeding
- budding
- blossoming
- pruning
- cultivating
- winter-rest
- reproducing

Explain:

Chapter · 5 ·

Staying Put

As the Father has loved me, so have I loved you. Now remain in my love.

John 15:9

AT ONE HUNDRED years of age, Hattie McConnell* has seen it all. Joy, sorrow, struggle, and victory. She has had moments of weakness and moments of strength. She's been through tragedy and tasted triumph. She's buried family members, faced widowhood, and prayed children into the kingdom of God. She's seen church at its best—and sadly at its worst. Faithfully she still attends church services Sunday morning and evening as well as a midweek meeting.

Member after member of our church will tell you that a Sunday highlight is to get there a little early, look for Hattie in her regular seat, and get one of her special hugs, a kiss on the cheek, a word of encouragement. Spend only a few minutes with her and you can see that she has learned a secret— the secret of staying put.

You see, Hattie has formed a habit—yes, a habit. She does so naturally what others find so difficult. She lives in His Word, worships in His presence, and trusts God completely.

---

* Since this writing, Hattie has triumphantly gone to be with the Lord. We rejoice with her!

Hattie knows what it's like to remain, to continue, and to dwell in her relationship to God. But Hattie's secret was not learned—or earned—at the age of one hundred. Hattie's secret was learned decades ago, and it's a secret all of us need to learn. Hattie is living proof that remaining or abiding in Christ is a permanent lifestyle worth developing.

A lifestyle based on abiding in God's love is an enduring lifestyle. It's the trademark of steadiness and rest, even when the winds of change blow around us. It provides a place to dwell and be comfortable in God's presence. Remaining in God's love is what helps us be at home among His people, enabling us to settle down and belong.

Remaining in Christ's freely offered love helps us live above our moods; it takes away the fear that God might change His mind about us. It gives us the assurance that God's love is eternal, that we can enter fully without fear of being expelled or excluded.

Stay put, His Word says. Remain. Be at home. Be established.

No barriers, no blockades between us and the Savior. No walls, no defenses. Just love. Lots and lots of love.

If we are ever to know God, it will begin with our accepting His love.

"Now remain in my love" (John 15:9).

————

In what ways are you more ready to receive God's love than you were at the beginning of this study?

What habits have you formed?
- keeping God out
- keeping Him at a safe distance
- staying somewhat near but not too close
- being close and friendly but not really intimate
- remaining continually in His love

Explain:

What habits do you need to change?

Define *remain* as used in John 15:9. If you were to incorporate that definition into your lifestyle, how would it help you change?

Section II
God Knows Me

O *LORD, you have searched me and you know me.*

PSALM 139:1

HE KNOWS ME. What a sobering thought. In spite of all the good impressions I've tried to make, all the good habits I've tried to develop, and all the times I've been convinced that no one really knows or understands me, I discover God knows me—really knows me.

How can God love me if He really knows me? Many Christians, including myself, find that a painful yet miraculous thought.

God knows you. Yes, really knows you. And what's more, He loves you. Incredible? Maybe, but true.

Chapter
· 6 ·

Hey, You!

But now, this is what the LORD says—he who
created you . . . "Fear not, for I have redeemed you; I
have called you by name; you are mine."

Isaiah 43:1

"HEY, LADY, you left your lights on," said the friendly but unsmiling man in the parking lot.

"Excuse me, ma'am, did you drop this?" said the polite stranger handing me my scarf.

"Where to, lady?" asked the cab driver.

How often we are nameless, unknown, and that makes us feel alone. And in this day of technology, we are often known, not by our given name, but by our account numbers, drivers' license number, and social security number.

Eager to be called by name, we look for somewhere to belong. But even then we often find a niche based on the impersonal: We are pegged by our ethnic heritage or slotted into a particular socio-economic group. We gravitate toward others who share similar interests or occupations; we hang out with those who possess the same gifts or talents. We stay close to those who perform the same function or have life roles similar to ours.

One can feel safe belonging to most any group. But being an "unnamed" member, though "safe," does precious little for one's relational needs.

Even when my husband uses his pet terms of endearment, calling me honey, sweetie, precious, or pal . . . nothing stirs me as deeply as when he pulls me close and whispers my name.

You see, my name personalizes me. It sets me apart from all others. Being called by name makes me feel acknowledged and recognized as a person, not just a role-player or a need-filler. My name makes me feel appreciated as myself.

God's Word says that He calls us by name. Not by account number (listing faults or shortcomings). Not by case number (listing problems). Not by skin color or income level. Not by education or accomplishments (or lack thereof). He doesn't call us by our abilities or talents or what we do for Him or the roles we play. He doesn't even use generic overused terms of endearment. He knows and uses the most personal, intimate word of friendship. God knows and loves—and calls you—by your name.

Listen to the voice of the Lord saying your name today. Just take a few minutes and listen with your heart; hear Him call you by name.

———————

How did your parents choose your name?

Have you ever learned the meaning of your name? If not, why not do it this week?

List several positive qualities that your name suggests.

Imagine what it would be like to have a personal appointment with God: He would sit close to you, look deeply into your eyes, and softly say your name. Is that a comfortable scene to you? Explain.

Chapter · 7 ·

The Real Me

> *The LORD searches every heart and understands every*
> *motive behind the thoughts.*
>
> 1 Chronicles 28:9

"WHAT'S IT LIKE to be Neva Coyle's daughter?"

Without a moment's hesitation, my daughter Rhonda opened her eyes wide and responded, "With or without makeup?"

It's true. No one knows me like my kids. I can cheerfully greet our friends at church, but my kids saw me at home getting ready for church and in the car on the way. Friends might see me laughing and friendly even late at night, but my kids see me when they wake me up in the middle of the night.

Yet even those who know me best may not know my insecurities and fears. I can hide my thoughts, temptations, and inner struggles from my family.

But with God it's another story. He's the only one who knows the basic, natural, unpretentious me. Even when I try to hide behind barriers, He knows; His knowledge goes behind them. He knows me though I am closed to Him; His love sees behind my locked doors.

Whether or not I recognize it, He knows me. Whether or

not I acknowledge it, whether or not I let Him work in me, He knows me.

As scary as it seems, it is good to have someone who knows—really knows—me. No pretense, no hiding, no need to conform to an acceptable code or standard of behavior. No false appearance or need to impress God. I can just be me—all that being me is, and all that being me isn't. No need to keep my guard up with God. No need to put on my makeup before my quiet time. It's not necessary to meet Him with a project or list of prayer requests in hand. I can just be me.

Even though God sees me at my worst, He knows and loves me better than any family member or best friend. And He knows and loves you, too.

He knows our strengths as well as our weaknesses. He knows our victories; He knows our defeats. He knows our abilities and also our inabilities. He knows our successes and equally our disastrous failures.

You see, He knows us—you and me—and He's not impressed. Not impressed with our achievement or depressed by our lack of it.

God knows what makes us do what we do and why. He knows what makes us make the decisions we make and why. He knows what makes us hurt and why, because He knows not only our personal history, but also our beginning (see Psalm 139). Not only our names, but also our natures.

He knows each person's character and how it is changing and being formed. He knows our personalities, our individualities. He knows our essence and singularity.

I like the fact that He knows how much I am like others and how much I am different from any other person on earth. I like the fact that He knows my disposition and my temperament and moods.

Think of it: The "me" no one else knows—not even my kids—He knows. He knows and loves me—just plain ol', little ol', insignificant me. And He loves me. Wow. What a miracle!

Name one person you think knows you better than any other. Name one thing that person does not know about you.

What is keeping you from sharing that one thing with the person who knows you best:
- fear of rejection or disapproval?
- shame or embarrassment?
- inability to be that open?

What does it mean to you to realize that God knows that which you cannot share with your most intimate friend?

What does it mean to you to realize that God knows you completely and loves you anyway?

Chapter · 8 ·

Getting Out–Going Through

*Let us then approach the throne of grace with confidence,
so that we may receive mercy and find grace to help us in
our time of need.*

Hebrews 4:16

YOU'VE BEEN THERE, maybe you've even joked about it.
More month than money, again.

You can probably identify with Sarah, whose whole family
just got over colds when her second grader broke out with
chicken pox, and the three younger ones hadn't had them yet.
Staring blankly, contemplating the probability of six weeks of
confinement, she lets the tears roll silently down her cheeks.

You may know how Jen feels. Fed up with ugly attitudes
and sexual harassment at work, she finally makes the difficult
decision that she will give her notice and look for another job.
Then, arriving at home eager to tell her husband, he makes
an announcement of his own: He's been laid off.

Maybe you can identify with Nancy, longing for someone
to listen to and care for her; for twenty years she's slept beside
a husband who feels like a stranger.

If you can identify with any of the above situations, welcome to the human race, which is like a club in which mem-

bership entitles you to a behind-the-scenes look at reality.

Need. Crisis. They eventually visit every household and affect every person.

Yet many of us live in need in one or more areas and survive; some even thrive in spite of it all. We all know those who are living examples of 2 Corinthians 4:8–9: "Hard pressed on every side, but not crushed; perplexed, but not in despair; persecuted, but not abandoned; struck down, but not destroyed." How can someone live above a crisis of need?

When faced with a situation of need, confronted with challenges that we can't just throw money at or bargain our way out of, it's time to learn the secret of going through the need—facing it—not just getting out of it. Sound strange? Maybe so, but true.

Daniel learned this secret the night he was tossed into a deep, damp hole in the ground. Once the lid was bolted in place, he discovered he was not alone. Lions shared his cell— *hungry* lions. I'm sure his first prayer was for rescue. But as the night wore on, he wasn't airlifted away. God didn't take him out of the experience. He took him *through* it. Sometime in the middle of the night Daniel realized that the lions were not going to attack—not even come close.

Recently I went through a difficult several months. I had a need—a crisis—that threatened to be my undoing. I prayed and asked God for rescue. Then I waited. I prayed again and asked for relief. And I waited again. Finally I earnestly sought the Lord and reversed the prayer. Instead of talking to God about my need, I asked Him to speak to me about it.

I learned several interesting things. I learned the difference between having a situation *fixed* and having my needs *met*. You see, I discovered I had a need to stretch my faith, to increase my trust in God and in His ability to provide. I needed to shore up the foundation of hope and depend on God—not *for* the answer but *as* the Answer.

At first, all I saw were the obvious needs, but He knew the not-so-obvious needs I had. It's so easy to exercise our faith and say that we're trusting God for a new house, a new job, or a new car when the present one is sufficient and the payments are being made every month. But it's when the pins are knocked from beneath us that our faith is *tested*. It's one thing to *practice* faith; it's quite another to live by it.

It's so easy to say, "Why worry?" when the worry isn't your worry. We're too quick to advise, "Don't struggle; just submit," when it's someone else's struggle. But we don't grow through someone else's need—only through our own.

God knows your needs, all of them. He's inviting you to trust Him, to go through your crisis with your eyes on Him, not on the need. He not only can provide for the need, the deepest need we have is for Him.

———

Read the following verses and write out a brief personal response to each.

Matthew 6:7–11: "And when you pray, do not keep on babbling like pagans, for they think they will be heard because of their many words. Do not be like them, for your Father knows what you need before you ask him. This, then, is how you should pray: 'Our Father in heaven, hallowed be your name, your kingdom come, your will be done on earth as it is in heaven. Give us today our daily bread.' "

Hebrews 4:16: "Let us then approach the throne of grace with confidence, so that we may receive mercy and find grace to help us in our time of need."

Philippians 4:19: "And my God will meet all your needs according to his glorious riches in Christ Jesus."

If you could see behind your obvious need to a deeper need, what would it be?

In what crisis areas are you trusting God to such a degree that there is no option apart from His meeting the need?

If God told you He wouldn't take you out of your present situation of need, but *through* it, how would that change your prayers or your attitude toward God? How would it change you?

Chapter · 9 ·

Known by the Hopes We Keep

*Against all hope, Abraham in hope believed . . . being
fully persuaded that God had power to do
what he had promised.*

Romans 4:18, 21

NO WAY. It's too late. It's impossible—useless. You're beyond hope. The mistakes you have made are fatal. Your life is beyond repair and your wounds beyond recovery.

Hopelessness—cruel, wretched, bitter hopelessness, threatening to squeeze every little spark of life and joy from your grief-stricken heart.

Abraham knew about disappointing impossibilities, but in spite of all the odds, he learned to hope.

Abraham had a word from God—a promise he was determined to see fulfilled. And against all hope, with hope he believed. Because he believed in the promise? No. Because he believed in the *Promise Maker*. He believed in God.

The promise had to do with the arrival of a baby, when Abraham and his wife were both well on in years. You see, God didn't command Abraham and Sarah to "go make a baby." He said He would *give* the baby (see Genesis 17–19). Abraham had to do his part, of course. He still had to be with

Sarah. But in the face of impossibility, Abraham would not accept the reality of futility; he accepted the promise of hope.

One thing I've noticed about Abraham. He didn't place his hope in what he promised God but in what God promised him.

We, too, can hope against all hope. You and I—we can learn to stop living by the promises we think we should be making to God and start hoping in the ones God makes to us.

Think about it: Somewhere within your soul there remains a tiny glimmering spark. Amid the smoldering remains of our shattered lives there is a glorious ember of expectancy stubbornly refusing to be denied its promise. When the blazing fire of disappointment dies down, gray coals of our dreams remain. And a small wind of hope excites the fire back to life.

Now, maybe for the very first time, you can step out in courage and place your hopes on something sure and solid: the Promise Maker.

Would you like to face tomorrow, hopeful, joyous, and free from doubt? God still has the power to do what He promised. Let hope in God and His ability sustain you. Against all hope, in hope believe.

———————

What's the difference between hopes based on my promises to God and hope based on His promises to me?

What promises has God made to you that you have thought impossible?

What would it take to revive those promises to you again?

If God said to you, "I know you. I know that ember of hope," what would He be referring to?

Chapter · 10 ·

Through and Through

O LORD, *you have searched me*
and you know me.
You know when I sit and when I rise;
you perceive my thoughts from afar.
You discern my going out and my lying down;
you are familiar with all my ways.
Before a word is on my tongue
you know it completely, O LORD.

Psalm 139:1–4

HAVE YOU EVER wondered what it would be like to have a friend who knew *everything* about you and still loved you? If you have ever wished for such a friend, keep reading.

It's not every day that someone comes along who has the ability to know us so completely and love us so freely.

It can be frightening to know that God knows us so well. From top to bottom, from beginning to end, from the inside out, He knows us.

Not one of our smallest notions has escaped His attention. He knows our lofty dreams and feels our bottomless disappointments. He witnesses our daydreams and sees every setback.

When we are encouraged and motivated, He is there. When we are disillusioned and uninspired, He is present. He can look in every corner of our lives, in every nook and cranny of our hearts, and see what we so carefully guard from public view, yet He loves us.

I don't know about you, but I'm glad there's Someone who knows me that well. My knowledge of His knowledge helps me be real to myself and more tolerant of others. I am comforted by the thought that nothing I do takes God by surprise; not one of my fiascos has caught God off guard. It is a relief to know that for all the secrecy I might attempt, when it comes to my Father God all pretense stops and openness begins.

I don't have to worry about God not loving me anymore, even when He knows the worst about me. You see, He knew the worst about me long before I was born. Even before my name rolled off my mother's lips, He knew how helpless I would be. And because He knew, He did something quite extraordinary—He sent His Son, Jesus.

God knows. Through and through, from stem to stern, from head to toe—He knows me; He knows you. And if that weren't quite incredible enough, His heartfelt passion toward you and me is love. Knowing all there is to know about us, His thoughts are toward us; His mercy is directly aimed at us, and His love pours out over us each and every day of our existence.

"But," you protest, "if He only knew. . . ."

Relax. He does. Someone knows who can love you no matter what. And the most amazing thing about it is: This kind of love wasn't our idea—it was His.

———

Recall an experience when you shared something deep and private and felt rejection because of it.

How have you transferred the fear of repeating that experience to your relationship with God?

What does realizing that God knows you so thoroughly do to the defenses you use to hold Him at a distance?

If God knows our every thought, why might He ask that we, as Christians, confess our sins to Him?

Section III

Being God's Friend

I no longer call you servants, because a servant does not know his master's business. Instead, I have called you friends.

JOHN 15:15

HAVE YOU EVER noticed that people who do a lot for others rarely let people get truly close to them? Try to do a favor for people who are always self-giving. Difficult, isn't it? They might not use the word *servant* to describe themselves in terms of their human relationships, but they might see themselves in that capacity. Always the helper, the fixer, never the one who accepts real friendship.

Might there be parallels in our relationship with God? We are so busy for God; we're caught up in worthwhile projects and service. Could it be that we have found a way to be around Him—involved in His work—yet safely distant from Him?

Perhaps we have been so disappointed by those who were supposed to be trustworthy that we have decided it's best to keep our distance even from God. If that is the case, we are missing a vital and wonderful depth of relationship God offers. While we are secure in servanthood, He is offering friendship. Why should we resist His friendly overtures a moment longer?

Chapter
· 11 ·

A Trusted
Friend

"Though the mountains be shaken
and the hills be removed,
yet my unfailing love for you will not be shaken
nor my covenant of peace be removed,"
says the LORD, who has compassion on you.

Isaiah 54:10

Do not let your hearts be troubled. Trust in God;
trust also in me.

John 14:1

PROMISES, PROMISES. We read them every day. We believe some, discount others. Companies pay big money for just the right advertising slogans or mottos that will instill trust in their brand names and products and services: guaranteed transmissions, dependable washing machines, experienced investment brokers. Then, when promises fail, we don't have far to look to find lawyers; commercials inviting us to trust them to get us a fair deal or settlement.

"If you can't trust us," said one leading retailer, "who can you trust?" But they were taken to court and fined for giving misleading information and repairs that weren't needed.

What do we do when something or someone we depended on disappoints us? How do we *go on* when someone we *counted on* doesn't come through? How do we recover when someone we believed in falls short of our trust?

Many experience betrayal and abuse—lives are violated and shattered. Tempting, isn't it, to pull our heads safely within our private, protected "turtle shells."

It's very scary to trust again when we have innocently trusted and been hurt or disappointed. It's not easy to trust God when we have devotedly trusted before and ended up being used.

What does God have to do to prove His credibility? Is it enough that He came to earth and walked among us in human form, taking upon himself our sins so that we have a way to cross the uncrossable canyon that separates God and us? That is enough, and yet He offers more: He showers us with the blessing of His abiding presence; He provides for our needs.

God is reliable and true to His Word. He is loyal, faithful, and unwavering in His love. He offers us a relationship that is stable and solid, based on His promises, not ours. He is as good as His Word and has proven it for thousands of years.

He speaks to us through the pages of the Bible, offering us proof of His identity, revealing His loyalty to His friends, and providing personal references of His approachability and trustworthiness. He offers friendship you can pin your hopes on, relationship you can put your faith in. Without a doubt, God doesn't offer just promises; He offers himself—a name you can really trust.

When all others fail, God cannot. When every other trust is violated, He maintains His. We can go on, overcome disappointment, and recover from painful betrayal because we can trust God.

———

When is it hard to trust God? Why is it hard to trust God?

In what area do you need to trust God right now?

In your own words, express your desire to trust God:

If friendship is a two-way street, in what areas might God be wanting you to be more trustworthy?

Chapter
· 12 ·

A Friend You Can Count On

No one will be able to stand up against you all the days
of your life. As I was with Moses, so I will be with you;
I will never leave you or forsake you.

Joshua 1:5

"AFTER THE DEATH of Moses . . . the Lord said to Joshua . . ." (Joshua 1:1). Can you imagine? Following years of serving under Moses's leadership, always hearing what God had said through another, suddenly this young leader hears God's voice directly. It must have made Joshua just a little nervous to be promoted to this position. Training, no matter how good and how long, never prepares one emotionally for that first day on the job.

As Joshua steps into his new position, God chooses just the right words: "As I was with Moses, so I will be with you." *You can depend on Me,* God was saying. *Over time I have proved I can be trusted.*

Entire industries have staggered under the suspicion that their products were not as dependable as others. Whole nations have reeled because their citizens could not depend on their leaders. Local churches, denominations, and the larger Christian community have suffered because leaders they counted on proved themselves undependable. Where do we turn when those we trusted let us down? How do we know God will not fail us as well?

Despite what you may have heard, God's reputation for being dependable is not shaken simply because some of His children aren't dependable. Yes, it's true. The God you trust is durable. You can depend on Him.

Trust is knowing that when you put the key in the ignition your car will start. Knowing that it will start day after day means relying on the car's durability and dependability.

Trust is knowing your friend will be there when you need her. Knowing that she will be there year in and year out, through thick or thin, good times and bad, means you rely on her durability and dependability as a friend.

Hebrews 13:5 reminds us of God's durable, dependable nature: "God has said, 'Never will I leave you; never will I forsake you.' "

How do we respond? "So we say with confidence, 'The Lord is my helper; I will not be afraid' " (Hebrews 13:6).

Moses depended on God. He said, "Be strong and courageous. Do not be afraid or terrified because of them, for the LORD your God goes with you; he will never leave you nor forsake you. . . . The LORD himself goes before you and will be with you; he will never leave you nor forsake you. Do not be afraid; do not be discouraged" (Deuteronomy 31:6, 8).

David trusted in God's promise of durability: "I [God] will not violate my covenant or alter what my lips have uttered. Once for all, I have sworn by my holiness—and I will not lie to David—that his line will continue forever and his throne endure before me like the sun" (Psalm 89:34–36).

God's love for you is durable and dependable. His care can be counted on day after day. The relationship you have with Him will stand up to any trial, failure, or discouragement you may have. His promises last a lifetime and longer. God will never let you down.

Am I claiming too much? I don't think so. You see, these claims are not based on my experience alone but on God's eternal Word. Not only can you trust Him, you can depend on His strength when you are weak and lean on His steadiness when everything around you is shaky. You can rest secure and safe in this relationship. He is faithful and true—completely dependable. You can count on it!

How has God proven himself to be dependable and durable to you?

God is One you can count on. In what ways do you let Him know that He can count on you?

Think of your relationships—with God, with yourself, and with others. In what areas have you been most durable and dependable?

Think of the people who depend on you. Do they know they can depend on God? Why is it important to help them understand that they can?

Chapter · 13 ·

True Friend

The LORD is righteous in all his ways
and loving toward all he has made.

Psalm 145:17

"THE REASON I AM HERE, Pastor, is because I know I can trust you." The woman twisted uncomfortably in her chair. "Your sermon on being nonjudgmental, and God's grace, has made be realize I can tell you what's bothering me. I know that whatever I tell you will be held in the strictest confidence and that you will not judge me." She dabbed at her eyes with a tissue. "This is so hard for me to say."

The pastor leaned back, settling deeper into his chair. Conscious that his body language needed to invite this troubled woman to talk about what was obviously bothering her so deeply, he uncrossed his arms and leaned forward again.

"I'm your pastor. I am here to help you, if I can."

"Well," she began slowly, "I'm not really here for myself."

"Oh?" said the pastor.

"No, I'm here for you."

"For me?"

"I believe your ministry could be so much more effective if you . . ." and she began a memorized list of changes the pastor could make that would suit her: ". . . cut the sermons by fifteen minutes; use less personal experiences, and quote more Bible. Furthermore, the congregation should sing more hymns instead of the contemporary style worship choruses. The choir should really have robes; the children's minister wears too much makeup. The youth pastor should shave off his moustache, and the ushers should smile and nod more at the people when the offering is being taken.

"I'm not really being critical here, I just know that this is what many people are saying. And I love you enough to make these suggestions to your face and know you will receive them in love." She dabbed at her eyes again. "I knew I could talk to you. Thank you for listening. I feel so much better now. Your counseling ministry is really your strongest suit, you know."

Wham! Rip! Slap! Stab! and she was gone.

This doesn't only happen to pastors. You and I have both had people who pretended to come in the name of the Lord to let us know that what is bothering them is *us*. We don't walk, talk, sit, or stand right. *Their* whole world would be better if *we* were different. Is it any wonder that we become suspicious and paranoid when we are approached?

Boy! If God's people are like that, how can I trust God? Simple. God is not like that.

God is authentic. When He says come close to me, He means He wants us close—simply close, nothing more. When He calls us apart to speak to us, it is because He wants to say something wonderful and life-changing. Only when we trust Him enough to say, "Examine me, my Lord. Show me what I need to change," does He intervene.

Of course there are those times when the Lord, through the Holy Spirit, lets us know when we are doing or involved with something we shouldn't. He brings conviction to us and gently leads us to repent and change. But, just because He beckons us does not automatically mean He has issue with us.

God doesn't approach us with hidden agendas or personal grievances. He comes to us with love and forgiveness, hope and life. He doesn't reach out with sweetness, and then squeeze the life out of us by harsh criticism.

Sadly, many never discover that God is always pure and

honest. They assume His character is like that of everyone who calls himself a Christian. Yet God keeps on loving, forgiving, drawing us to himself, proving that He is faithful and that His motives are only for our good.

———————

Recall an experience when someone approached you deceptively and wounded you.

Are you blaming God for that encounter?

How have you used past experiences with people to keep you from getting close to God?

How can you change that tendency?

Chapter · 14 ·

Remembering

And he took bread, gave thanks and broke it, and gave it to them, saying, "This is my body given for you; do this in remembrance of me." In the same way, after the supper he took the cup, saying, "This cup is the new covenant in my blood, which is poured out for you."

Luke 22:19–20

RELATIONSHIPS BEGIN with openness, deepen with discovery, and solidify through communication. They are strengthened with commitment and can even be sealed with vows, as in wedding ceremonies. But there is another dynamic to relationship that we often overlook—remembering.

It does a relationship good to share memories. To think back to tough times made easier by being together. To look back at triumphs that would have been tragedies if faced alone. Remembering those special times that strengthened the relationship keeps two people aware of the importance of each other over the long haul.

Anniversaries, birthdays, and family gatherings often prompt thoughts of the past. Though choices and circumstances may separate loved ones, memories help us maintain our roots and identities.

Shared but fading experiences become sharp and vivid with mutual recollection. One person remembers details another has long forgotten.

Jesus knew how important remembering is to a relationship.

One night, eating His last supper with His friends, He took some bread, blessed it, and passed it around the table. He said, "This is my body given for you; do this [eat this] in remembrance of me" (Luke 22:19). Then He took a cup, blessed it also, and passed it to His friends: "This cup is the new covenant in my blood" (Luke 22:20).

While speaking about the future, He created a memory, not only for the few friends gathered there that night, but also for those of us who through the next centuries would also become His friends.

"Remember," Jesus said. "Recollect, recall."

It is easy to get so busy that we don't take the time to remember what Jesus has done for us; He has brought us into new life in Him. It's important to remember—to take the time to think back, not to dwell on a tarnished, regretful past, but to rejoice that it is gone, never to haunt or threaten us again. When we take time, as He did with His disciples, and reflect on His broken body and His blood spilled unselfishly for our sins, we keep our identification with Christ alive and fresh.

Communion services are special times for Christians, but do we ever take the time to find a quiet place all alone with Jesus and remember Him in this way? I invite you to take a small cracker and a swallow of juice and go to a private place. Then, all by yourself, unhurriedly recall what the Lord Jesus has done for you.

Sit for a few moments with the cup and the bread in front of you and contemplate His goodness. Remember His blessings and recall several times when He has answered your prayers. Read Luke 22:19–20 and restate it as a commitment of remembrance. Take the piece of bread or cracker, hold it up to the Lord, and say: "Lord Jesus, I take this bread and remember your broken body and thankfully receive the healing and hope it represents for me." Eat it.

Then take the glass or cup, hold it up, and say: "My Lord and Savior, I receive the cleansing your blood was spilled to provide for me. Thank you for doing for me what I was unable to do for myself. I accept free access to God, which you have given me through the sacrifice of your life."

As you drink, let the reality of what God has done in sacrificing His Son for you wash over you anew. Let the reality of Christ in your life bring you new hope and life. Be identified with Him in a new, deeper—yes, more personal—way, through remembering.

How or why is remembering hard for you?

Why do you resist taking time alone for reflection?

How does remembering help you establish your identity with Christ?

Name one blemish or sin you are glad to have covered by the blood of Christ:

Chapter
· 15 ·

Never Alone
Again

I will praise the LORD, who counsels me;
even at night my heart instructs me.
I have set the LORD always before me.
Because he is at my right hand,
I will not be shaken.
Therefore my heart is glad and my tongue rejoices;
my body also will rest secure,
because you will not abandon me to the grave,
nor will you let your Holy One see decay.
You have made known to me the path of life;
you will fill me with joy in your presence,
with eternal pleasures at your right hand.

Psalm 16:7–11

"DON'T LEAVE ME!" My greatest childhood fear was that my parents would abandon me. If left with a relative, I was terrified that my mother wouldn't come back. Nothing anyone said could make the gnawing feeling go away: Someday I would be forsaken. No one knew how to assure me that I wouldn't someday be discarded or disowned by those I loved.

At five years old I went to school *knowing* my mother wouldn't be there when I returned. That thought stayed central in my mind all day.

Teachers wrote notes home saying that I was preoccupied, a dreamer, sad. I didn't dare tell anyone why—it would only hasten what I perceived to be my tragic destiny—that someday I would be abandoned.

I outgrew my fear of physical abandonment but retained another deep fear. If my parents weren't going to send me away, they would someday stop loving me and emotionally withdraw. What a terrible way for anyone to live, especially a child.

This fear has crippled me in many ways even as an adult. You see, I transferred this fear to God. I knew He loved me; He had to; after all, He loved the whole world. But, though He would love me as part of the group, certainly He couldn't love me as an individual. This line of thinking made it seem essential that I stay part of the group God was sure to love. I was driven to "perform"—to make sure I belonged.

I was overextended and overcommitted to church responsibilities and activities.

Then I was still afraid I'd be left alone physically; I watched the clock every afternoon, fearful that my husband would be killed on his way home from work.

I was a Christian—a forgiven, born-again Christian—but filled with fear I lived as an orphan trying to find or even create a family and a place to call home.

Then it finally began to sink in. God's promise of His presence was not for groups, per se, but for people. Individuals —you and I—can live unashamed, unafraid, and secure in His presence.

To compensate for my fears of being abandoned, forsaken, and left behind, I was trying to earn—to merit—living in His presence. Fearful of not fitting in or of being neglected, I tried to make a place for myself and find an identity that God would accept. Little by little I discovered through reading the Bible that living in His presence drives those same fears away. What joy came when, through study of the Word, I found that God had given me an identity in Christ that made a place for me and allowed me to be my unique, God-created self.

Once I let myself *belong*, based on the merit of Christ's death for me and His life in me, I no longer had to work at fitting in.

I experimented with allowing myself to be aware of God's constant presence in my life. I challenged my fears by spending even more time in His Word, by taking time to be silent before Him, by experimenting with conversational, "Hey, God" prayers as opposed to formal, "Our Father, which art in heaven" prayers.

The more I allowed a personal relationship with God, the closer He felt to me. The closer He felt, the more secure I became with expressions of praise and affection toward Him.

The more I expressed my love for Him *to Him*, the more confidence I found to do the things He directed me to do.

No longer afraid of being abandoned, I have gained the wonderful freedom to be alone—which has given me the joy of being a writer. No longer feeling like an outsider, I am happy meeting new friends; I welcome new experiences. No longer adrift in fear, I am able to determine clear goals and direction.

Knowing that God loves me and wants to be near me has freed me to live close to Him and sense His precious presence. I am conscious of His nearness. I no longer live as an orphan but as an heir—a child of God who will never leave home.

"No one will be able to stand up against you all the days of your life. As I was with Moses, so I will be with you; I will never leave you or forsake you" (Joshua 1:5).

———————

When have you experienced fears of abandonment?

How are your close relationships affected by this fear?

Has God ever let you down? If you feel He has, talk to Him about this. What is His response to you?

How can you choose to be more aware of God's presence today?

Section IV

Knowing God Changes Our Relationships With People

Let us hold unswervingly to the hope we profess, for he who promised is faithful. And let us consider how we may spur one another on toward love and good deeds. Let us not give up meeting together, as some are in the habit of doing, but let us encourage one another—and all the more as you see the Day approaching.

HEBREWS 10:23–25

THERE'S A GREAT big troubled world out there. But then, I don't have to tell you that. You live and work in it every day.

You walk right beside people who are out of touch with the concept of God, much less know His love. You work among cynics and feel their strife. You speak daily with those plugged into dog-eat-dog competition and feel the pressure that their attitude puts on your own performance. You feel their stress, and fight against taking it on yourself—as do I.

In our troubled world, battling individual histories of pain and disappointment, it is understandably difficult for many to make friends.

One missionary wrote these words home: "The needs of the people are overwhelming. The loneliness and isolation we feel threatens us every day. Yet we realize that the needs of the people are why we're here, and the loneliness was not an unknown factor at home."

Written by a friend, those words ministered to me. He was learning how to set aside his own pain in order to minister to the needs of those around him.

If we ever come to really know God, it will deeply change the way we view others. Knowing Him gives us a new perspective of those who know Him as well as those who don't. And a new awareness of others changes our understanding of God.

Chapter · 16 ·

The Ministry of Reconciliation

All this is from God, who reconciled us to himself through Christ and gave us the ministry of reconciliation: that God was reconciling the world to himself in Christ, not counting men's sins against them. And he has committed to us the message of reconciliation. We are therefore Christ's ambassadors, as though God were making his appeal through us. We implore you on Christ's behalf: Be reconciled to God.

2 Corinthians 5:18–20

WE LIVE IN a fractured world. Nation is pitted against nation. Ethnic group against ethnic group. Race against race. Employees against employers. Government against private enterprise. Women against men. The "right" against the "left." We even face church splits and fragmented families.

In this climate of differences that divide people from each other, in this world of sin that separates people from God, we Christians are given the ministry of reconciliation. Overwhelming? You bet it is. That's why we must turn to our relationship with God as a foundation as we move into this much-needed ministry.

Where do we start? By getting involved. But how? Well,

some say, write your congressman. Change a local ordinance.

Yes, but— What's the "but"? You see, it is easier to target a cause than to be involved with a neighbor. It is much less threatening to write a letter to a senator or newspaper editor than to befriend a person who might inconvenience us with a need.

I'm not advocating that we stop trying to let our voice be heard—not at all. We should target causes and write letters whenever we can, but, while we protest, let us not forget the neighbors and strangers who need the presentation of Jesus and His love. Remember the woman up the street and the man across the way who are hurting.

In the same way that we must never give up speaking our voice in the social and political arena, let us always be alert to those around us who need our ministry of reconciliation.

Let us win them over to our dearest Friend—the Lord Jesus Christ. Let us be willing to help them when they come to terms with their need of Him. Let us be involved with people—helping them resolve their conflicts within themselves and with others.

Those of us with the ministry of reconciliation are bridge-gappers, difference-resolvers, and mediators. Our ministry is a sacred calling, our holy orders. And it's based on and empowered by our ever-deepening relationship with the Triune God—Father, Son, and Holy Spirit—the God who reconciled himself to us.

We need to take seriously the call to be instruments of God's love—ambassadors of Christ's kingdom, recruiting officers for God's army.

Will I accept the call? Will you? If not us, who?

Who was the last person you purposely befriended who had overwhelming needs, and seemingly nothing to give you in return?

When you retreat from someone in need, what is the most likely excuse you find for being uninvolved?

If you were to think of one person who needs your God-given ministry of reconciliation, who would it be? Write out a prayer here for that person's need as you see it from your vantage point:

Write out a prayer offering yourself as an instrument of God's love to that person:

Chapter · 17 ·

Peacemakers

*Blessed are the peacemakers, for they will be called
sons of God.*

Matthew 5:9

I DON'T HANDLE conflict well. Neither does my friend
Myrna. Yet I have watched her as she has reached out at great
personal expense to repair a relational bridge in need of res-
toration.

Laying her entire heart open, she seeks peace and pursues
it. She steps into the difficult issues and makes herself vulnerable. She states as simply as possible her perspective and
keeps at it until she sees some progress toward reconciliation.

Barb is like that, too. Open and frank, she has often been
an ambassador of peace.

And there's Marieta, such a conciliator and diplomat.

You would think that with such expert peacemakers in my
life, I would learn.

But for all the role-model peacemakers right before me,
sadly I am more of a *peace keeper* than peacemaker.

I would rather claim "love covers" and hide my hurt and
difference with someone rather than do the hard emotional
work it takes for resolution. It is easier for me to conceal my

feelings than to work through them.

I would prefer to keep things on an even keel—not rocking the boat—than to confront. Protecting the status quo is more appealing to me than paying the emotional toll required for growth and change.

Fortunately Myrna, Barb, and Marieta have not settled for the little peace-keeping efforts I have offered; they have extracted much more from me. I'm thankful to them for helping me become more aware of being a peacemaker.

They have encouraged me to share my inner feelings about snags in our individual relationships. They have pursued me when I have withdrawn into myself and confronted me when I have thrown up walls of defense and curtains of doubt.

My peace-making friends not only listen to me wail and cry about my troubles, but they also tell me when I've wailed and cried quite enough. They have encouraged me to work through my problems instead of running from them. They have required me to grow when I wanted to whine instead. Peacemakers? Yes, indeed.

Peacemakers who knew that my peaceful facade sometimes hid deep inner turmoil. Peacemakers who were willing to risk friendship with me when they sensed static in my relationship with God and others. Peacemakers who didn't stop at pacification but pushed for reconciliation. Peacemakers who wouldn't settle for appeasing me—but pressured me toward peace until I embraced it for myself.

Thank God for peacemakers; peace keepers like me need them—desperately.

Are you a peacemaker or a peace keeper? Do you generally prefer self-protection or problem solving?

Name a friend who is experiencing a lack of peace. Peace-makers leave a person intact. What measures can you take that will promote peace but leave this person intact?

Describe a peace-making experience that went sour. What went wrong? How can you avoid those same mistakes again?

If you were to ask God to change you into a peacemaker, how do you suppose He would begin?

Chapter
· 18 ·

Unity

*My prayer is not for them alone. I pray also for those
who will believe in me through their message, that all of
them may be one, Father, just as you are in me and I am
in you. May they also be in us so that the world may
believe that you have sent me. I have given them the
glory that you gave me, that they may be one as we are
one: I in them and you in me. May they be brought to
complete unity to let the world know that you sent me
and have loved them even as you have loved me.*

John 17:20–23

When we're "lumped together," we try to make the best
of it. We stay to our side of the sanctuary, carefully select
which committees we volunteer for, and choose projects that
put us together with those we like and understand. But God
didn't call us to make the best of it. He has called us to live
in unity.

Don't be taken in by those who preach *sameness* as unity;
recent religious fads have spawned a whole host of pale imitations. Everyone thinking or looking alike or talking the same
lingo is not unity; it's uniformity. You can look alike, walk
alike, and even hold to the same teaching but be out of unity
with one another.

God has called us to be one in Christ; living together we become a whole. Our individual uniquenesses joined together create a harmony—each of us singing our own part yet blended together with many different parts. Can you imagine how boring a symphony would be if every instrument had the same sound and all played the same part throughout the whole piece?

Yet we pressure people to fit in and to become "just like us," instead of appreciating the richness that comes as many differences blend together—one in Christ.

Think of the artist's palette—a variety of paint colors to create shades of many hues. But if every color were mixed entirely into every other until all the properties of each were lost, you'd have a muddy mess. You will have lost the shades of the rainbow. And the painter will have lost the ability to create a vivid, colorful work of art.

The apostle Paul uses yet another image to illustrate unity: a physical body that works as a unit but with many specialized parts—hands, feet, ears, teeth, knees.

We are not called to blend our personalities. We're not called to be the same, but to be together, shoulder to shoulder. To join forces and work side by side. We grow together, strengthen and support one another as we pull together.

Unity is that special cooperative effort we make when we become intent on a single purpose. It happens as we empty ourselves of our selfishness while preserving our uniqueness. Unity is at its best when we grace each other instead of grumble.

Unity happens among those who base their identity on Christ, who base their worth on the price paid at Calvary, who are willing to submit their unique gifts for the good of the whole body of Christ.

One, yes. But different *ones* combined together to make a difference that only the whole can make as it works as a unit.

———————

In your group or church, what is the biggest obstacle to unity?

Think of someone whose gifts and talents differ from yours. How might God use your gifts to complement this person's gifts?

How has this understanding changed how you feel about that person?

If you were to see harmony rather than uniformity as a mark of unity, how would that change you and your approach to group or committee projects?

Chapter · 19 ·

Walking in Love

*It has given me great joy to find some of your children
walking in the truth, just as the Father commanded us.
And now, dear lady, I am not writing you a new
command but one we have had from the beginning. I ask
that we love one another. And this is love: that we walk
in obedience to his commands. As you have heard from
the beginning, his command is that you walk in love.*

2 John 4–6

INFLUENCE. I have it and so do you—whether you realize it or not. What we do and don't do influences others. It's staggering to realize what an impact my lack of determination or season of indifference may have on someone else. But it's true.

What kind of people make up the church of Christ, anyway? Who are we, this people of great influence, working side by side and harmonizing our gifts and merging our efforts? Of course we have the obvious differences—young and old, male and female. But we have other differences, too.

Some might be called "upscale"; others would be labeled "simple and plain." Many are serious and expect others to be. Some of us play as hard as we work. We are both educated and uneducated, bright and slow. We include the curious as well as the content, the active and passive. Our numbers also include the affluent and the poor, achievers and plodders. Many of us are goal oriented while others are people oriented. We are doers on one hand and "ride-alongers" on the other.

The whole includes the hurting, and for every thoughtful person we know, we could name a careless one.

But one thing we have in common is Jesus. And when we have Him as the cohesive characteristic of our relationship, we have something unique, something that goes beyond co-existence, even beyond tolerance or togetherness: We have love for one another.

There is an affection and esteem we hold when we walk in love toward one another. We care and are kind. We extend the benefit of the doubt in a disagreement. We treasure another in spite of our differences.

Among Christians none need feel uncherished and unwanted, unappreciated and unloved. The church that walks in love is full of loving, friendly folk waiting at the door, ready to roll out the red-carpet treatment for any who come to look us over.

The church is brimming over with warmth and acceptance. The redeemed people of Jesus Christ are cordial to visitors, and goodness is written across their smiling faces. They carry a soft spot in their hearts for the unsaved and demonstrate unswerving patience toward new Christians.

Oh really, you say, is the church so perfect?

There's no such thing as a perfect church, just a perfect Savior and King. As for the church, it's in process. Not fully there yet, but we're working on it.

Reflecting upon Christ's perfection, the imperfect church is learning to reach the world instead of trampling over one another. We are learning to make a difference in our dying society instead of cornering fellow believers with trivial complaints and grievances. We are seeing the need to reverse the tide of evil instead of quarreling over droplets of differing opinions.

Released from judgment, we release others from ours. No longer held as bond-slaves to sin, we extend to others the same hope for freedom in Christ as we have. No longer tied to lists of performance requirements, we extend to a desperate world the love and hope of a better way—the only Way, Jesus.

And we do it in a very simple way: As we abide in Christ, His love for us nourishes the fruit of love for others.

Name one fellow believer whom you graced with love (rather than judged) within the last month.

Name someone who has walked in love with you instead of getting even.

What can you do to make yourself more aware of God's love for you and for those who naturally grate on your personality?

Write a prayer, asking God to give you opportunity to pass on His love to someone who particularly needs a reassuring word.

Chapter · 20 ·

Compassion

Jesus went through all the towns and villages, teaching in their synagogues, preaching the good news of the kingdom and healing every disease and sickness. When he saw the crowds, he had compassion on them, because they were harassed and helpless, like sheep without a shepherd. Then he said to his disciples, "The harvest is plentiful but the workers are few. Ask the Lord of the harvest, therefore, to send out workers into his harvest field." He called his twelve disciples to him and gave them authority to drive out evil spirits and to cure every disease and sickness.

Matthew 9:35–10:1

"WHO NEEDS IT?" the young woman asked somewhat belligerently. "All this religious stuff is nothing but a crutch. I learned a long time ago not to need anyone or anything." But a glimmer of a tear gave away her pain.

Who needs it? She does. Yet she's right in one sense: It's not religious stuff she needs; it's Jesus. Not another list of rules and regulations—a relationship. And she can admit her need only if someone cares enough to touch her with the love and compassion demonstrated by Jesus.

Compassion never makes a grand entrance or bold statement. It begins with simple manners and consideration. It grows into graciousness and goodness. It fully develops into tenderness and mercy.

Lonely, hurting people need to be touched by compassion, as do those who feel displaced and abandoned. Brothers and sisters who are ill need more compassion than sermons on faith. Those who have failed need compassion not pep talks.

Sin-trapped people need the loving touch of a forgiving Savior. The hopeless need to be wrapped in the hope of His compassion.

How does He intend to do this? Through us. Yes, you and I are the compassionate hands of Christ. We're the compassionate touch He uses to heal, mend, and win those who need Him.

As Jesus commissioned His disciples to minister compassion, the Spirit calls us to extend His lovingkindness. We're the long-suffering, understanding listener so many are looking for. We're the tenderhearted, gentle representatives of a living, loving Christ. We are the ones with the mission of mercy.

Why did He choose us? We know what it feels like to be hopeless and wounded beyond repair. We remember what it was like to have only darkness and doubt crowding our minds and blinding our pathways. We can identify with the poor and hungry of spirit. But as we have learned of Him, as we have abided in Him, we have been nourished by the life-changing power of His love and compassion.

Those of us who have walked through great pain and remember how far we have come are often most compassionate. To those who struggle we are less apt to respond with a sharp "Snap out of it!" We who know what it is like to be greeted with the narrow, suspicious eyes of the pious often more easily open our hearts in friendliness.

We who know the love of Christ are the ones who will make a difference. We will see the young woman's defiant "Who needs it?" change to a prayer admitting her need. We will be there when another new life is born into the kingdom of God.

Name someone in your circle of friends and acquaintances who needs compassion.

What kind of compassion does this person need?
- pity
- tenderness
- sympathy
- kindness
- mildness
- gentleness
- patience
- concern
- understanding
- tolerance
- mercy
- graciousness
- forbearance
- friendliness
- comfort

How can you show compassion to this person?

Since beginning this study, how have you changed? How has the change in you changed how you view your place in the body of Christ?

Section V

People Who Know God Change

---

*F*or I will take you out of the nations; I will gather you
from all the countries and bring you back into your own
land. I will sprinkle clean water on you, and you will be
clean; I will cleanse you from all your impurities and
from all your idols. I will give you a new heart and
put a new spirit in you; I will remove from you your
heart of stone and give you a heart of flesh. And I
will put my Spirit in you and move you to follow
my decrees and be careful to keep my laws.

EZEKIEL 36:24–27

PEOPLE WHO KNOW God, who abide in Him, are people who change. They become more like Him. You can see it in their actions. In their face. You can see the fruit that matures in their lives—the lush, fleshy fruit of the Spirit.

Those changes that come in our relationship with Christ influence how we see Him, how we perceive ourselves, and also how we see and relate to others.

Chapter · 21 ·

Enablers of the Very Best Kind

Encourage one another and build each other up.

1 Thessalonians 5:11

I HOPE YOU have a Millie, as I do. She knows just what to say when I am discouraged and overwhelmed. She has a knack for lifting the wet blanket thrown over my plans and ideas when someone has put a damper on my enthusiasm.

It's hard to get the jump on Millie. I try—but no matter how I try to sneak up on her with a word of appreciation, she always has a well-spoken compliment for me that she seems to have saved for just that moment.

No matter what, she always has a ready hug and an encouraging word. She seems to know all the little behind-the-scenes things that need attending to, and you often can find her cheerfully working alone to finish the tasks others have overlooked or chosen not to take on.

Millie is an expert at a pat on the back, and her sweet disposition inspires everyone she knows. She can cheer up a room just by walking into it. She is a true-to-life encourager.

I can't help but think that Paul must have had people like Millie in mind when he told the early church to encourage one another.

Contrast the encouraging Millies with those whose main function seems to be to cast a pall on vision. How different the Millies are from those who throw cold water on hopes and dreams, who try to talk us out of our courage and question our motivation.

Who are the encouragers who are ready to say, "Hey, I think that's great"? They're those who have been so touched and changed by their relationship with God that they have learned to love His friends no matter who they are and what they look like.

I don't know about you, but I couldn't make it without those who encourage me. Yet I wonder, *Do I encourage? If my attitude walked in before me, would I brighten up a room I entered? Am I free with pats on the back? Am I ready to boost another or cheer someone on?*

You know, Millie is not only my encourager; she is my model. She gives me not only someone to look up to, but also a challenging example to live up to.

Lord, let my life be so touched, and let me be so changed by your life in me that I can be an encourager, too.

Name someone who encourages you. How or why does that person encourage you?

Think of someone who discourages you. Why or how does that person discourage you?

Which do you let have more power in your life, the encourager or the discourager?

Name someone you know who could use some encouragement. In what creative way could you provide that encouragement?

Chapter · 22 ·

Touches of Tenderness

Praise be to the God and Father of our Lord Jesus Christ, the Father of compassion and the God of all comfort, who comforts us in all our troubles, so that we can comfort those in any trouble with the comfort we ourselves have received from God.

2 Corinthians 1:3–4

I COULDN'T SEE her face clearly—because my eyes were filled with tears, because my heart was sick with pain. Yet before I could utter the simplest words of explanation, her outstretched arms encircled me. Not a word of advice. Not a similar personal experience. Nothing but my name was needed or spoken. My friend simply held me and let me cry. Comfort, plain and simple—welcome comfort.

When life is at its bleakest, there is nothing to compare with someone who knows how to comfort. When circumstances are at best dismal, only a comforter will do. It's a comforter you need when life hands you the dreariest news.

Comforters cannot practice; they are simply those who have been so deeply touched by the power of God and their relationship with Him that they instinctively reach out at just the right time, speak very little, and touch a heart breaking with pain.

You know, I can't even remember exactly what caused so much pain that day, but one thing is sure, I will never forget the comfort of my friend.

Am I a comforter? I must run a self test to see. How about you? Maybe we're both due for a "comforter check."

Check-up question number one: When someone shares a painful experience, does it trigger sympathy and compassion? Or does it trigger a memory I can't wait to share with the hurting person? (You know, the "you think that's bad, wait till you hear what happened to me!" syndrome.)

Check-up question number two: When meeting a person in obvious pain, do I want to run in to be with that person so I can share the pain—or so I can fix it? Comforters know they can't fix the pain, but that doesn't prevent them from reaching out to share it. (Some people just stay away from the pain: "I didn't go to see Sue when her husband died because I just didn't know what to say." Or, "I can't stand to visit Marlene in the hospital; I just don't know what to do at hospitals." Sound familiar?)

Check-up question number three: When confronted with another's pain, do I compare it with my own to see if it's worth bothering about? ("What's she whining about? She should have my problems, then she'd have reason to go on that way.")

Check-up question number four: If I am to comfort with the comfort I have received from the Lord, how do I explain my tendency to avoid comforting or being comforted? In other words, why do I withdraw when in pain—or from those in pain?

If you were to become a comforter, what personal risks would you have to take?

If you were to resist becoming a comforter, what personal loss might you risk?

Chapter · 23 ·

Togetherness

Submit to one another out of reverence for Christ.

Ephesians 5:21

"WHEN I'M EIGHTEEN, I'm outta here!" How many parents have heard that statement—and how many of us said it when we were seventeen?

Independence! How we wished for the day when we could be our own boss, free from parental rules and restrictions. Longing to loosen the fetters, we talked big about the day we would prove we could make it on our own. We were sure we could face the world and its challenges without help from anyone. It's the American way, isn't it? Wanting little or no help from parents, we set out to carve a self-centered path that we were sure others would envy.

Little did we know that this American characteristic of independence would leave us lonely and isolated.

Is it any wonder that verses that deal with "one another" leave us perplexed and fussing? Take Ephesians 5:21, for example. We spend so much time discussing the semantics of *submission* that we totally miss the concept of "one another."

Love one another; be kind to one another; bear one another's burdens—all assume a kind of togetherness that is foreign to our independent thinking. Detached and remote, we stand far off and ponder how we can do that "together stuff" and still maintain a separate identity and our precious distance.

This is where learning to know God and to take the risks of loving His friends begins to carry a high price. We might have to give up some of our aloofness. We might have to become bonded—even attached—to one another. We might even grow to rely on others to round out our sense of purpose and meaning.

Indifference could change to caring. Caring might lead to involvement. And if we become involved, we might have to consider one another—even step out of our safe, cloistered fortress.

Those of us who have discovered that we need others have also discovered that the "ideals" of self-sufficiency and standing on one's own two feet are empty lies.

The submission I'm suggesting is not the kind that makes you jump through hoops or insists on blind obedience to abusive authority. I'm talking about the value of relationships among God's friends in which each person's gifts are acknowledged and appreciated. An atmosphere that encourages the balancing of people's strengths and the covering of people's weaknesses. Relationships that respect differing opinions and give deference to another's preferences. Relationships in which love is the regulator and caring is the governing rule.

I am convinced that there can be relationships in which two or more people are so secure it is not an issue of who gets his or her way. In these relationships parties are more interested in keeping in step than in getting ahead. Friends stand shoulder to shoulder rather than competing to see who gets what first.

Joy, Judy, Janet, and I can all tell you that there can be distance in miles yet close communion of heart among friends.

And yet too often a five-foot church aisle becomes an uncrossable chasm. Why? Because that good-old American independent spirit—dare I say self-centeredness?—has never given way to mutual submission.

How about you? When it comes to the church of Christ, are you a lone ranger or a member of the team?

When was the last time you went to a church function just to be together with other Christians?

What characteristics of your friendship with God could give you confidence or courage to reach out in friendship to other Christians?

What can you do to break down one barrier between you and a potential friend?

Make plans to call a specific friend, just to grab a few minutes of "togetherness" with no particular issue to discuss.

*Bless those who persecute you; bless and do not curse.
Rejoice with those who rejoice; mourn with those who
mourn. Live in harmony with one another. Do not be
proud, but be willing to associate with people of low
position. Do not be conceited.
Do not repay anyone evil for evil. Be careful to do
what is right in the eyes of everybody. If it is possible, as
far as it depends on you, live at peace with everyone. Do
not take revenge, my friends, but leave room for God's
wrath, for it is written: "It is mine to avenge; I will
repay," says the Lord. On the contrary:
"If your enemy is hungry, feed him;
if he is thirsty, give him something to drink.
In doing this, you will heap burning coals
on his head."
Do not be overcome by evil, but overcome evil
with good.*

Romans 12:14–21

THERE ARE THOSE times when getting "a little satisfaction" is so inviting. My guess is that I'm not so different from you. We both know how secretly gratifying it is to see someone

117

get her "just desserts" or "get a taste of his own medicine." We can probably think of someone right now who "could use their comeuppance."

But wait, what about verses such as these in Romans 12?

How can we redirect negative vibes toward someone we'd like to hit back? How can we change our attitude toward someone we'd like to see get a little of what he has dished out? How can we live at peace with those with whom we'd rather settle a score? How can we survive the unreachable expectations of those who are the most critical and impossible to please?

As we get to know God, we learn that He is surrounded by a group of friends who have not yet become who He wants them to be. We brush elbows with the immature and sit on committees or even live with people who irritate us. Right within our small Bible-study or support groups and churches— our fellowships—we can fight our biggest battles and experience our deepest wounds. It ought not to be so; I agree. But there is a vast difference between what ought to be and what is.

When we learn to walk in love among God's friends, the following strategies will help us not only to survive, but also to grow and thrive. They will help us become more like Jesus through dealing with the realities of what *is* while we press on in hope toward what *ought to be.*

"Honor one another" (Romans 12:10). Nothing disarms a loaded chip on the shoulder faster than honoring. Proverbs 17:9 says, "He who covers over an offense promotes love, but whoever repeats the matter separates close friends." Since it runs counter to our purpose of loving God to promote separation, let our strategy be to promote closeness by covering offenses with love. This has nothing to do with trying to figure out who does or does not deserve love or forgiveness. It may not even make much sense, but, remember, this is a strategy, not satisfaction. This does not mean that you become a doormat for every thoughtless, careless person you know. But it can mean that you have learned to overcome in such a way that no one gets hurt.

"Bless those who persecute you" (Romans 12:14). It is such a foreign thought—to bless someone when it would be more

natural and normal to strike back, or, in common terms, to punch 'em out. But Proverbs 12:20–21 says, "There is deceit in the hearts of those who plot evil, but joy for those who promote peace. No harm befalls the righteous, but the wicked have their fill of trouble." We don't bless those who persecute us so we can prove our righteousness or their wickedness but to preserve our joy and protect ourselves from the harm others would inflict upon us. You can't cause the wicked any more harm or pain than they are bringing upon themselves.

"Do not repay anyone evil for evil. . . . Do not take revenge" (Romans 12:17, 19). *Boy,* we grimace, *it would seem so right, even understandable to get even.* Yet 1 Peter 3:9 says, "Do not repay evil with evil or insult with insult, but with blessing, because to this you were called so that you may inherit a blessing." We don't have a score to settle, nor do we have to dose someone with her own medicine. We have a purpose— a call far beyond any emotional wounds we may want to avenge. We have an inheritance to guard, a blessing to preserve. Our strategy to reach that purpose is purposely *not* to get even. No sweet revenge? Revenge is not our job, nor is it in our best interest. It is in our best interest to learn to overcome. Revenge, no matter how sweet it may be at first, will last only for the moment and leave its regrets deeply imprinted on our hearts. Overcoming with love will last forever, with no lasting regrets, only the imprint of a loving, forgiving Savior stamped forever on our personalities and attitudes.

"Do not be overcome by evil but overcome evil with good" (Romans 12:21). Even when others put impossible expectations or conditions on us, we can overcome. When we have been hurt deeply or persecuted because of our skin color or gender, we can overcome. When unspeakable horrors have been inflicted on us, we can overcome. And we can do it with goodness—God's goodness.

As 1 Peter 4:8 says: "Love each other deeply, because love covers over a multitude of sins." What a wonderful strategy for loving God's friends, even the unlovely ones.

———

Within the past few days I had an opportunity to cover someone's sins with love. Sadly, I blew it. Can you identify with such an opportunity? Briefly describe:

I know how I could have handled that situation differently. What are some of the ways you could have better handled your situation?

We will probably have such an opportunity again. How can we be ready?

Chapter · 25 ·

Giving Freely

Share with God's people who are in need.
Practice hospitality.

Romans 12:13

DAY AFTER DAY, we count on the generosity of God. We do it in as many unconscious ways—perhaps more—than conscious. We depend on Him for the simplest, yet most basic requirements—like the air we breathe. We depend on Him for the right mixture in the air around us, providing just the right amount of oxygen to keep us alive.

We depend on the fruit of the earth for food, and furthermore, we depend on Him to see to it that the food we eat sustains us and provides us with the energy we need for happy, productive lives. But we depend on His generosity for far more than just our physical needs.

We also depend on His free grace and His abundant forgiveness. We count on His never-ending love and boundless mercy. We crave His approval and presence for our lives.

Can you imagine a selfish, tightfisted God supplying only enough oxygen to barely keep you alive, but not enough to keep you conscious? Or, can you think of what life would be like if the food we ate every day suddenly turned rancid? If the water we drank turned bitter at the tap? We can't even begin to think of the devastation to the quality of our day-to-day lives and standard of living should God suddenly decide to withhold His generosity and hospitality toward us. We are guests here on the earth—God's guests. And He's proven to be a generous and gracious host.

Yet, are we afraid to believe in the generosity of God when it comes to His mercy? Do we think of His grace being poured out in miserly portions? Do we live our lives as though God would scrimp on His love and tenderness toward us? Do we hold back in our requests before Him as if He were stingy and pinching every blessing, rationing them out in meager measures? Do we pray as though His ability to answer is barely sufficient?

No, of course not! We know God is kind and gracious. We have discovered Him to be open-handed and genuine in all His dealings with us. We have explored His whole-hearted warmth and lavish provision for our needs. We have known His love to be without measure, and His interest in us to be without distraction, restriction, or expectation of our performance.

Because of His dealings with us, we can also be generous, given to hospitality with one another. We are the given, giving. The blessed, blessing. The loved, loving. The fed, feeding. The befriended, befriending. The graced, being gracious.

Living a free, generous life, we no longer keep track of social obligation, or count on return favors. We are free to live and love without demanding reciprocation. Reaching out, not always waiting to be reached. Because I am convinced that God will provide and that He loves me and cares for me, I can freely and without reservation also care—and so can you.

This is a wonderful way to live. Open-handed, open-hearted, open-minded, and forgiving. We don't treat one another as though we are performing some perfunctory duty or live as though all we are capable of is shallow, superficial relationships. We genuinely love and care for one another deeply. We pursue hospitality and radiate with friendliness toward those around us. We maintain approachability and openness toward one another.

We do, don't we? Isn't this what we as Christians are like?

———————

When was the last time you had a new couple or family in your church over for dessert and conversation?

When was the last time you offered to watch someone's children so they could go to a retreat or go out for an anniversary dinner?

What about offering to baby-sit for a young couple at church who are involved in ministry or would like to be?

When was the last time you offered to be a greeter at the door of your church?

When was the last time you talked to your neighbor?

How could you be more "given to hospitality"?

What could you do about it today?

Section VI

The Vine Life

———

As the Father has loved me, so have I loved you.
Now remain in my love.

JOHN 15:9

"STAY HERE," I warned my children when they were little. "Stay in touch. Call me," I tell them now that they're grown. What am I saying? Stay close. Don't wander away.

That's what the Lord is saying to you. Stay in my love. Don't let circumstances or difficult relationships come between you and me. *Remain*, He says, *Remain in my love.*

That's where your security is. That's where you'll find insight to His Word. Close to Him, living, remaining in His love—that's where you'll sense His presence and experience His care. That's where life is.

Chapter · 26 ·

For Sure, For Sure

For I am convinced that neither death nor life, neither
angels nor demons, neither the present nor the future, nor
any powers, neither height nor depth, nor anything else in
all creation, will be able to separate us from the love of
God that is in Christ Jesus our Lord.

Romans 8:38–39

I know whom I have believed, and am persuaded that he
is able to keep that which I've committed unto him.

2 Timothy 1:12, KJV

YOU HEAR THEM every day. Promises of dependability, high performance, and quality. Assaulted with such promises and finding many of them empty, we grow calloused and suspicious, even immune to their allure.

Catchy phrases such as "Raise your hand if you're sure," "the dependability people," or "a good tree to come to for shelter" have lost their punch. We aren't sure we're in good hands with anyone.

Life has handed us a generous measure of difficulties that have left us insecure, wretchedly vulnerable, and seriously doubtful. We experience hostile work environments, face alarmingly unstable financial futures, and feel uncomfortable with our political leaders, both local and national.

Can we have faith in anything when everything seems so dangerous, even hazardous? Can we commit to something or someone without risk? With our very identities hanging by a thread, can we ever feel secure again?

Yes. Indeed, yes!

Words like *safe, protected,* and *sheltered* can find their way back into our vocabularies, our hearts, our experiences. We can find the pathway to stability and walk with firm emotional and spiritual footing.

Through building a deep relationship with our loving heavenly Father, we can be secure. We can know what it's like to live in a safe shelter. Through relationship with Him we can experience unquestioned love, closeness, and attachment.

Living under the Father's watchful eye of love, care, and guidance, we can feel at home, anchored. There, out of danger, we can let His love cover and heal our wounded emotions, our damaged sense of personal worth. Once again we can take deep breaths of hope and promise, letting them revive our weary spirits.

Why? Because only He is believable. Only He has proven himself over and over again to be completely dependable.

No longer do we have to find reasons or seek permission to exist. No longer do we have to strive for a sense of worth or love.

We no longer have to find a faith, because as we are rooted in Christ Jesus faith finds us. No longer do we have a need to base our security on how well we keep precise legalistic teachings or find our identity in belonging to a particular denominational group. We live in Him. We find our future in Him. We find our worth and our identity in Jesus Christ and His sacrificial love for us.

This is the abiding life. Rooted, growing, budding, blossoming, and bearing fruit—abiding in Him. It is at this level that our ever-growing knowledge of God continues to deepen. Our intimacy with Him grows sweeter and our hope burns ever brighter.

We belong to Him. He belongs to us. We're a family, and we stick together.

How do you measure your worth?

What makes you feel worthwhile and productive?

How does the intimate, abiding life with Christ invite you or threaten you?

Think over your plans for the next forty-eight hours. How will the intimate, abiding life of Christ affect your relationship with other Christians?

Chapter · 27 ·

Living the Word-Life

How can a young man keep his way pure? By living according to your word.

Psalm 119:9

WOW! WHEN YOU least expect it, there it is again. Sin, blatantly exposing itself on our billboards and television programs, in our magazines—boastfully displaying itself through people locked in its deadly grip. Life in the nineties is overstocked with immorality, violence, and dishonesty. "Reality" television programs take us right into the centers of crime-ridden cities or drug-infested communities.

In schools, teens are handed condoms for "protection"; teaching abstinence in sex education classes is frowned upon or termed "unrealistic." Children are carrying guns and knives to school.

Entire financial institutions have crumbled because of greed and dishonesty on the part of wheelers and dealers. Internal affairs departments are busy investigating our law enforcement agencies—leaving many to wonder who is investigating the internal affairs departments.

We live in a sinful and perverse generation. Sin is flooding our cities, rural communities, and even finding its way into our churches. Yet the Bible shows us a way to live in the world while keeping ourselves pure. Sounds incredible, doesn't it? But it is possible.

Psalm 119:9 asks the question we all ask at one time or another: How can I step through the muck of sin that surrounds me and yet remain pure? The answer is found in the succeeding verses.

"I seek you with all my heart; do not let me stray from your commands" (Psalm 119:10). These days we don't talk much about wholeheartedness. In fact, it runs counter to our culture, which teaches us to hold back some, if not most, for ourselves while giving to others a minimal "feel-good" portion.

But if you ever learn to know God, it will be because you have chosen to come to Him with your complete and entire heart. Nothing held back, nothing in reserve.

"I have hidden your word in my heart that I might not sin against you" (Psalm 119:11). I have an entire Bible stored in my computer. I just press a few buttons, and the verses I want to insert into this book appear instantly on my screen. The Bible is there in my computer because I put it there. But the Bible stored in my computer is only handy to my work; it really does not help my life, my heart.

I want my heart to have the Bible stored in it, so that pressing just a few internal buttons brings appropriate verses to mind for application to my present situation. If the Bible is to be there for instant retrieval, it will be because I put it there. Memorizing is hard for me but essential if I am to have a hope of keeping my life pure. (Are you like me: slipping into a pattern of underlining or highlighting verses instead of memorizing them?)

"Praise be to you, O LORD; teach me your decrees" (Psalm 119:12). A pure life comes from a teachable heart. It does not mean that I have never done wrong in the past. It does not mean that I will be perfect in the future—only that when I stumble, through repentance I come back for more instruction and teaching.

"With my lips I recount all the laws that come from your mouth" (Psalm 119:13). Nothing reinforces my commitment to purity like talking about it—not about how good I'm doing but about the goals I have and the hope I have for doing better.

"I rejoice in following your statutes as one rejoices in great riches" (Psalm 119:14). Grumbling gets me nowhere fast. My attitude makes all the difference. I can choose my attitude. If I rejoice in following God's ways and living according to His Word, it is because I have chosen to do so.

"I meditate on your precepts and consider your ways" (Psalm 119:15). Taking time to meditate on God's Word takes effort. I work hard all day and am tired at night. So I make a commitment to get up early each morning, making the time I need to ponder God's biblical promises and instructions. Thinking through the application and direction I need, well, it simply takes time. But time well spent!

"I delight in your decrees; I will not neglect your word" (Psalm 119:16). Then I do it all over again. By that I mean that a commitment to a biblical lifestyle is an ongoing daily discipline. This discipline has kept me from sin, shown me the way back when I have sinned, and even warned me of avoidable danger ahead.

The pure life is possible. It is not a life of legalistic perfection but of perfect peace. Not a life of unrealistic expectations that I won't stumble but the promise of strength to get up when I do. It does not mean that I will live without flaw but that I can take those flaws to Christ the moment I am aware of them, expose them to His love, and by the power of the Holy Spirit become an overcomer.

This is a life of hope, not of performance. A life full of promise, not exactness. This wonderful life in Christ—relating to our loving God—is a life of worth and discovery. And He gave everything He had to give it to us.

Compare several seasons in your life—when you did have consistent daily devotions and when you did not.

Recall an experience when a memorized passage of God's Word sustained you through difficulty.

If you were to choose to memorize a passage of the Bible, what would it be? Make specific plans to start memorizing that passage.

Chapter · 28 ·

ICU
Intimate Care
Unit

After leaving them, he went into the hills to pray.
When evening came, the boat was in the middle of the
lake, and he was alone on land. He saw the disciples
straining at the oars, because the wind was against them.
About the fourth watch of the night he went out to them,
walking on the lake. He was about to pass by them, but
when they saw him walking on the lake, they thought he
was a ghost. They cried out, because they all saw him
and were terrified.
Immediately he spoke to them and said, "Take courage!
It is I. Don't be afraid." Then he climbed into the boat
with them, and the wind died down.

Mark 6:46–51

WE CHRISTIANS ARE funny people. We come to God in
response to His love and accept His Son into our lives and
hearts. From then on, we tend to focus on our love for Him;
we act as if His love for us ended with our salvation. Then,
out of our love for Him, we seek our place of service. We
express our love to Him in taking a Sunday school class or by
singing in the choir. We take our turn in the nursery at church
and show up on special work days. All of which is good, as far
as good goes.

But we must be careful. At this point we can become professional Christians rather than practicing, growing believers. We become seasoned and experienced, accomplished, and many times authoritative. Veterans at this way of life, mastering service and commitment, we are in danger of forgetting that the Lord loves us more than we could ever love Him.

We can start to believe that we are the ones with the vision, that God has to be convinced that we have the right program and plan. Our prayers become more like proposals than friendly conversations. Bolstered by our talent and imagination, motivated by our creativity, we can discover ourselves over our heads in programs, overwhelmed to the point of despair. Discouraged by the lack of commitment of others, we soon feel as if we have been abused, not only by other Christians, but even by God.

Too often, we "strain at the oars" of responsibility. With the wind against us, we use every bit of energy just trying to keep our little boat afloat; in the effort we lose sight of the destination and long for the security of a port, any port!

Then what? We often seek an immediate rescue, desperately in need of spiritual first aid. It's time to check into the ICU—the Intimate Care Unit—where Jesus himself is the Physician on duty.

Look for Him. He will probably appear where you least expect Him. Most of us are guilty of thinking He is standing on the dock ahead, waiting for us to arrive, when really He is walking right beside us. When we see Him that close, we can feel afraid and ashamed that He sees us in such need. Sadly, many of us, instead of being grateful for His presence, feel guilty for needing it.

Words from the Lord, given to others in their times of need, are also for us today:

"The LORD watches over you—the LORD is your shade at your right hand; the sun will not harm you by day, nor the moon by night. The LORD will keep you from all harm—he will watch over your life; the LORD will watch over your coming and going both now and forevermore" (Psalm 121:5–8).

"He fulfills the desires of those who fear him; he hears their cry and saves them. The LORD watches over all who love him" (Psalm 145:19–20).

136

"The LORD is good, a refuge in times of trouble. He cares for those who trust in him" (Nahum 1:7).

"He tends his flock like a shepherd: He gathers the lambs in his arms and carries them close to his heart; he gently leads those that have young" (Isaiah 40:11).

Also read Psalm 55:22 and 1 Peter 5:7.

Do we believe it? When we experience the ups and downs of life and the struggles we encounter as we serve the Lord, do we realize how much He cares for us? Do we reach out in appreciation for His ability to rescue us, or do we feel guilty for needing His help? Do we focus our attention on our shortcomings, or allow ourselves the adventure of experiencing His intimate care? Are we so preoccupied with what we perceive to be a failure or a disappointment to God and others that we miss His desire to attend personally to our needs?

Whatever you're straining against, no matter how stormy your voyage, stop. For this divinely appointed moment, experience God's care. Don't listen to the wind of opposition and struggle. Jesus wants to say, "Take courage! It is I. Don't be afraid." Won't you let Him get into your boat? If you will, the storm will soon calm and the sea will once again be smooth. The destination will again be in sight and your course set aright.

Recall a time when you felt more guilty about needing God's help than appreciative that He was willing to give it. Why do you feel guilty?

How can you welcome God's care into your situation today?

What words could you use to invite Him to be intimately involved with your present circumstance? Write them down:

Jesus
and
~~Me~~ We

I am the vine; you are the branches, if a man remains in me and I in him, he will bear much fruit. . . . . If you remain in me and my words remain in you, ask whatever you wish, and it will be given you.

John 15:5, 7

SOMETIMES YOU RUN across a verse that seems to be such a simplified version of the Christian life in Christ that it could almost be reduced to a formula. However, after further thought, the above verse, while appearing to contain the very heart of the Christ-life, has a far-reaching impact upon our daily lives, extending even to our relationships.

Each of us has been tempted at times to pull back into Christ, as it were, desiring to live with and for Him alone—even to the exclusion of others. Do you ever get tired of people? Do you become weary of their problems and worn out from miscommunication? I do. We have been hurt by criticism and carry emotional scars from misunderstanding. We want to retreat within the safe boundaries of a loving, caring relationship with Jesus—alone.

However, whenever we do that, we discover that the very

life of Christ that He desires to pour back into us during those quiet retreat times is really the strength and skill to deal with people. Living in union with Christ *the Vine Life* is a fruitful, productive life. It makes a difference in me, of course, but the difference doesn't benefit me alone, it spills over into the lives of those around me—into my relationships.

Once we grab on to Jesus, allowing our life to be totally grafted into Him, we discover a new identity. We call it, in the Christian circles I am a part of, "who I am in Christ." We speak with authority because of "who I am in Christ." We pray in His name because of "who I am in Christ." However, we speak very little of "who *Christ* is in me." "Who I am in Christ" speaks of how my life is different because I am in Jesus. But, "who Christ is in me" speaks of how *I* am different because He is in me. If my being in Christ changes *my world,* how does Christ being in me change *me?*

Remaining means *bearing,* not just existing at some wonderful level of spiritual enlightenment. *Abiding* and *producing* are inseparable concepts. Living a life united in Christ means a life that is growing. Dwelling in Him, continuing in Him, standing firm in our identity in Christ produces new life not only in me, but through me to others.

"Stay," the Word invites, then yield a harvest. Abide in Him, then bud, blossom, flower, and propagate.

It is interesting to note that the fruit of the Spirit is not so much to benefit the one in whom it is manifested, but the fruit of the Spirit—love—is to benefit our relationships. Joy, peace, patience, kindness, goodness, faithfulness, gentleness, and self-control are what make our relationships healthy and strong.

I have said all this to say one simple thing—there is no such thing as a personal, private relationship with Jesus Christ that does not benefit our human relationships.

When we understand that knowing Jesus Christ not only makes a difference in us, but a huge difference in our relationships with others, we begin to lay down our expectations, requirements, and demands of those relationships. Our real expectation is in God. Our genuine hopes lie in Him. Our needs can only be truly met by Him.

All of our contact with others is affected by our abiding in

Him. Not only will the fruit of the Spirit be manifested in us, but it will touch all our relationships as well.

———————

What fruit of the Spirit do you see forming in your own life recently?

How it is affecting a specific relationship?

What emotion do you see surface most often when you face conflict?

What fruit (see Galatians 5:20) needs more growth in you when that happens?

The apple isn't nourished at the branch, but at the root of the tree—in what ways can you do more to nourish your life at the root?

Chapter · 30 ·

Whole and ALIVE

Remain in me, and I will remain in you. No branch can bear fruit by itself; it must remain in the vine. Neither can you bear fruit unless you remain in me. I am the vine; you are the branches. If a man remains in me and I in him, he will bear much fruit.

John 15:4–5

IT'S TIME. If you sincerely want to join the small handful of people who know what it is to be whole and ALIVE, it is because the Word of God has found a place in your heart and application to your life.

I have invited you to take a giant step in your relationship with God and learn to know Him at a deeper level. To explore the personal impact a deeper relationship with your heavenly Father can have on your devotional life and on your relationships with other Christians. To discover how your relationship with God can be enjoyed and counted on during the tough times as well as the good. To capture the exciting vision of yourself in intimate relationship with Jesus Christ. I have invited you to recognize and embrace the "vine life" of John 15.

Simply stated, I have encouraged you to see God as your Savior *and* Friend.

It has been my prayer that you experience wholeness as you deepen your relationship with Him. That you sense a foundational security in knowing Him. That you know His tenderness toward you.

My hope is that you have formed new concepts of how lovingly God sees you and that you have also seen Him in a new way. That the *fear of the Lord* has changed from a personal terror to an appreciative awe and enjoyment of His majesty and beauty, His loving heart.

I hope you've committed to God the scars from early childhood that left you feeling worthless. That you have found new purpose in your life and sense His care and concern for you.

It is also my hope that you have found new meaning in human relationships—that as you have decided to be united with Christ as closely as the branch is united to the vine, those relationships are bearing sweet fruit.

This study has presented an opportunity for a lifetime of meaning and fulfillment—united with God, connected to His friends. But don't just take my word for it—find out for yourself.

How has this study changed the way you define your relationship with God?

How has it changed the way you perceive human relationships?

How can you continue the work begun in your heart during this study?

Name a change you have consciously made after reading this book:

Leader's
Notes

GROUP GUIDELINE SUGGESTIONS:

This study may be used in several ways. First, as a personal devotional study without help from a leader or a group. Second, by partners or in a home or neighborhood Bible-study group with planned discussion questions and prayer time. Third, this material is adaptable for use in an already formalized group such as a women's ministries group or a Sunday school class.

When used individually, the study can be completed in thirty days. When used in a group setting, one section should be covered individually in the week between meetings, where insights can be shared and questions found in these leader's notes can be discussed.

A good group approach to this study is one of personal investigation and shared responses. Discussion questions will help bring out even more insight into application for personal growth.

Because the material covered may delve into personal areas, do not expect or force everyone to participate each time. Encourage even the slightest participation with affirmative comments, regardless of the contribution.

Because this is a responsive study, there are no wrong answers. Through the study, you will get to the heart of many emotional issues. Some people in your group may desperately need a listening ear, and a correction from you may discourage them from participating in your discussions or even attending your group. Allow the Holy Spirit to do the correcting and give you the grace of patience and sensitivity.

If an individual monopolizes the conversation or goes off on a tangent, carefully approach that person afterward and ask if you can be of help individually. During the study there may be a dramatic breakthrough, where one person will draw the attention of the group to herself and her needs exclusively. That would be the exception, however, not the rule.

If someone in your group asks a question, don't take the responsibility upon yourself for always having the answer. Allow others in the group to provide input as well. In fact, let others respond before you give an answer.

There are three basic rules that you should strive to keep throughout the study:

1. *Start and end on time.* Everyone is busy. Set your meeting times and stick to them. One and one-half hours works well for evening groups. Daytime groups may meet a little longer. Actual study discussion will take only a portion of that time. Fellowship and sharing prayer requests help develop strong bonds within your group. Make time for that to happen.

2. *Begin and end with prayer.* The opening prayer can be a simple blessing on your time together—much like asking the blessing before a meal.

A second prayer time might address the needs of friends and family of the group. You might have everyone write down the name of a person they are concerned for and a very brief statement of the need on a small slip of paper. The slips can be placed in a basket and redistributed to the group. Each person takes a request and prays a brief sentence prayer concerning the person or need.

Closing prayers can be centered around the individuals' needs related to the study and the discussion questions. As leader, you might close the meeting in prayer.

3. *Involve everyone.* Some of the issues covered in this study are very personal. Given the amount of abuse and misunderstanding some in your group may have experienced, they may not be ready to enter into much discussion. But the fellowship time, prayer, and other group responsibilities may help build trust and an openness. Find a way to involve even the most reserved person in a way that is comfortable and safe.

There may be times when you are unable to get through all the discussion questions provided. In your preparation time, check a few you consider essential for your group and always try to end with the last question provided.

DISCUSSION QUESTIONS

Section I: The Challenge of Change

Read together the introduction on page 16 and then use the following questions for discussion.

1. How do you perceive intimacy with Christ as a practical part of the Christian experience?
2. Suggest some of the hindrances to having an intimate relationship with the Lord.
3. What difference does personalizing John 3:16 make in how you view your relationship with God?
4. What differences are there between the relationship God offers and the relationships that have hurt you in the past?
5. What are the differences between your relationship with God and the best human relationships you have ever had?
6. Name some reservations people might have about intimacy with God.
7. What is your new understanding of Jeremiah 31:3?
8. How has the analogy of the garden flowers helped you understand being "rooted" in God's love?
9. Do you think some can use the resting or "winter season" in their relationship with God as an excuse? How?
10. Give a personal example of "checking out on" God rather than remaining in His love.
11. How can this group help you choose to remain in His love?

Section II: God Knows Me

Read together the introduction on page 38.

1. What do you know about the history of your name? How did your parents choose your name?
2. If you could have chosen your name, what would it have been and why?
3. What was your emotional reaction to imagining God being very close to you and softly saying your name?
4. How does the fact that God knows you thoroughly make you feel?
5. God loves you in spite of what He knows about you. How does this motivate you to change?
6. What is the difference between "getting out of" and "going through" a difficult time? How does this relate to your life right now?
7. Why do you suppose people lose hope?
8. What do we have to do to base our hope on God's promises?
9. How can this premise (basing hopes on a word from God) be abused?
10. Read Psalm 138 together. What special application does verse 8 have to our hopes?
11. Knowing God knows us through and through, why do we keep Him "at arm's length"?
12. God knows you completely. What does this mean to you personally, privately?

Section III: Being God's Friend

Read together the introduction on page 60.

1. How do we know we can trust God? Why is it so hard?
2. What is the difference between trustworthiness and dependability?
3. How do you know you can depend on God?
4. Have you ever had an experience similar to the one told about the pastor in chapter 13?
5. Have you ever deceptively approached someone? How did you feel later?
6. Not everything presented as "truth" is truth. Explain.
7. Read John 1:9. If we know that God is faithful, why might we still avoid confessing our sins to Him?
8. Sharing our faith is sometimes awkward, and we may shy away from traditional "witnessing." If we think of evangelism as simply introducing one friend to another, how would that change the way we approach telling others about Christ?
9. How can we introduce our friend Jesus to our unsaved friends if we have none? Name one unsaved person with whom you might build a friendship.
10. Where do feelings and fears of abandonment come from in your case?
11. When is it easiest to feel as if God has abandoned you?
12. How can you be secure in His presence?
13. How might taking our relationship with God to the depth outlined in these first three sections affect our human relationships?
14. What is your biggest hindrance to building strong human relationships?

Section IV: Knowing God Changes Our Relationships With People

Read together the introduction on page 82.

1. In your own words define *ministry of reconciliation.*
2. Who has been a "minister of reconciliation" to you?
3. How can this group help you fulfill the calling to be a minister of reconciliation?
4. What's the difference between being a peacemaker and a peace keeper?
5. Comment on the following verses:

   "Peacemakers who sow in peace raise a harvest of righteousness" (James 3:18).

   "There is deceit in the hearts of those who plot evil, but joy for those who promote peace" (Proverbs 12:20).
6. Working together gets things done. Then why do we experience strife rather than unity when we attempt to work together?
7. What inner changes do you need to make to better contribute to unity in your group or church?
8. If your church or group were to embrace the biblical concept of walking in love, what immediate changes would you expect to occur?
9. If believers would walk more in love, how would that impact our world? (Refer to John 13:34–35.)
10. When have you seen a lack of compassion in your own heart?
11. How have you determined to be more compassionate?
12. What new ministry or area of service for you could come out of what you have learned so far in this study?

Section V: People Who Know God Change

Read together the introduction on page 104.

1. Recall an experience in the past (while protecting identities of groups and individuals) in which you were specifically discouraged by someone. Speaking in general terms, tell why you were discouraged.
2. In a group like this one, there are usually some natural encouragers. Who has encouraged you and why?
3. What can we do to *purpose* to be encouragers without being phony?
4. What is the most effective expression of comfort you have experienced?
5. It is hard for some people to accept comfort. What are such people missing?
6. What is a person missing who has never been a comforter?
7. How have we been trained to be independent?
8. What is so hard about being mutually submissive?
9. Can you remember an experience when you got even? What was the effect on you personally? How did it change that particular relationship?
10. Has someone ever "covered" for you? How did that change your relationship with that person? How did it change you?
11. Does our culture encourage or discourage hospitality?
12. Why are we tempted to stay uninvolved in people's lives?
13. How does the church reflect our uninvolved American culture? How does it differ?
14. How could we be a part of a necessary change, to pursue hospitality?

Section VI: The Vine Life

Read together the introduction on page 126.

1. Define *abiding* and relate it to a personal or physical experience.
2. How does being exposed daily to advertising slogans and promises cause us to be cynical toward God's promises?
3. How can we maintain our sensitivity toward God's Word, His love, and one another while the assaulting world "toughens our skin?"
4. How can Bible memorization help us maintain a pure life?
5. If anyone has memorized a passage this week, please share your progress with the group. Why did you choose a particular passage?
6. Comment on the point in chapter 28 about feeling guilty for needing God's intervention. How have you experienced it?
7. Share a personal experience—a "non-crisis" time when you were aware that God was caring for you.
8. Define the *vine life* of John 15:4–5.
9. What relationships within this group have budded or grown because of this study?
10. As a group, take communion together. Take a piece of unleavened bread or cracker. As you share it with the others, express your feelings toward the Lord and the group. Then take juice, share it together, and express what the blood of Christ means when it is applied to your relationships—past, present, and just beginning.
11. Pray together.